About t]

After graduating from Trinity College, Cambridge with a degree in Classics, Martin Fone started his working career as an audit assistant. However, he soon found the world of bean-counting too racy for his taste and retreated to the calmer pastures of the insurance industry. He had a successful business career, during the course of which he co-authored two books on public sector risk management, which were adopted by the Institute of Risk Management as their standard text books.

Perhaps it was his acquaintance with the murky world of the financial services industry that piqued his life-long interest in the psychology of scams and hoaxes.

Since retiring, Martin has had the opportunity to develop his interests, mainly reading, writing and thinking or, as his wife puts it, "locking himself away in his office for a few hours a day". In particular, he has been blogging and writing in his tongue-in-cheek, irreverent style about the quirks, idiocies and idiosyncrasies of life, both modern and ancient.

This is the third book he has written since leaving the insurance industry behind, following on from *Fifty Clever Bastards* and *Fifty Curious Questions*, both of which, he says, are still available from all good book retailers and high-class charity shops.

FIFTY
SCAMS
AND
HOAXES

Martin Fone

Matador
9 Priory Business Park,
Wistow Road, Kibworth Beauchamp,
Leicestershire. LE8 0RX
Tel: 0116 279 2299
Email: books@troubador.co.uk
Web: www.troubador.co.uk/matador
Twitter: @matadorbooks

ISBN 978 1789015 775

British Library Cataloguing in Publication Data.
A catalogue record for this book is available from the British Library.

Printed and bound in Great Britain by 4edge Limited
Typeset in 11pt Bembo by Troubador Publishing Ltd, Leicester, UK

Matador is an imprint of Troubador Publishing Ltd

This book is dedicated to my parents, Ray and Brenda.
I am also eternally indebted to my wonderful wife, Jenny,
whose love and support made this book possible.

CONTENTS

PART 2 FINANCIAL SCAMS

PART 3 HOAXES

INTRODUCTION

"The origin of the diddle is referrable to the infancy
of the Human Race. Perhaps the first diddler was Adam."
- Edgar Allan Poe - *Diddling: Considered as One of the
Exact Sciences* (1843).

I AM FASCINATED by scams, how they are constructed,
rolled out, the psychology they deploy and the final
outcome. Perhaps my interest is grounded in something
deeper. Maybe it's the fact that most scams rely on the
interplay between three of the less desirable human traits:
avarice, credulity and gullibility.

Many people believe that credulity and gullibility are
the same thing, but there are distinct differences, albeit of
degree. Those who are credulous are willing to believe
something, even in the absence of reasonable evidence,
but, generally do not act on that information; whereas

someone who is gullible is the easier to dupe because they are prepared to act upon such information.

To illustrate the point, if I believe a man can squeeze himself into a wine bottle, I am credulous. But if I rush out and buy a ticket, convinced that I will see a man squeeze himself into a bottle, I am gullible (see the Great Bottle Hoax of 1749, No 44).

As Stephen Greenspan noted in *Annals of gullibility: why we get duped and how to avoid it* (2009), what differentiates gullibility from credulity is the coupling of action with belief. "Gullible outcomes", he writes, "typically come about through the exploitation of a victim's credulity."

This may all be a bit too sophistic for some, but what is clear is that when credulity and gullibility clash with avarice, the fall-out can be quite spectacular.

Those who perpetrate frauds typically prey on one of our two major insecurities: our health and our wealth. We like to live in good health and we want to feel that we have enough money to live comfortably. When we suffer ill-health, we like to get our hands on some drug, tincture or potion, which is going to alleviate our symptoms and restore us to rude health. We are also on the look-out for ways in which we can extend our financial assets, preferably in a way that involves as little effort on our part as possible. Unfortunately, there are some people who see these natural desires as something to exploit.

Advances in medical science are such that we tend to forget that, in the 19th century and earlier, a visit to the doctor was not only expensive but downright dangerous. Those, who had a medical problem, would often resort to old wives' medicinal cures or those peddled by quacks, a term abbreviated from the Dutch noun Kwakzalver, meaning the hawker of salves, to find solutions. There was no shortage of strange potions, which claimed to be a panacea for all ills. In was not until the Pure Food and Drug Safety Act of 1906 that 'doctors', working in America, were forced to act in a responsible manner.

The First Epistle to Timothy (Chapter 6, Verse 10) contains the sage warning, "for the love of money is the root of all kinds of evil." In the second section of this book, I provide a number of examples of the grief, mayhem and despair that greed and love of money can bring with it. I have eschewed the obvious examples of financial skulduggery. I have chosen to highlight lesser known and, perhaps, more colourful tales of financial malpractice, mainly from the 18th and 19th centuries. The old adage, "if it looks too good to be true, it probably is", is one that is usually best remembered when deciding on an investment strategy for your personal finances.

Not all scammers exploit human credulity and gullibility for financial gain. The book concludes with some of my favourite hoaxes, where the perpetrators displayed mind-boggling ingenuity to test the boundaries of these lamentable human traits.

Confidence tricksters were known as diddlers in Edgar Allan Poe's day after James Kenney's character, Jeremy Diddler, who appeared in the farce, Raising The Wind, published in 1805. In his analysis of diddlers and diddling Poe identified the following attributes; audacity, focus on smaller crimes, self-interest, ingenuity, perseverance, impertinence, originality, and a grin.

Across the spheres of medicine and finance, we will certainly come across examples of some or all of these characteristics. Other common features, which we will see time and again displayed in our picaresque collection of scammers include; incredible claims, extensive and creative use of advertising, which play on people's fears and aspirations, unscrupulous business practices and, when it all goes wrong, as it often does, a propensity to flee the scene and leave others to pick up the pieces.

An enterprising financial journalist in the 19th century could do no worse than travel back and forth on the cross-channel ferry. It was packed with fleeing fraudsters!

I hope you will find the examples of the scammer's art interesting – there is sure to be something for everyone.

Part One

Medical Scams

THE DEMON DRINK

I ADMIT IT. I like a drink or three. Despite regularly exceeding the so-called safe alcohol unit guidance, I do not consider that I have a drink problem.

Since time immemorial Homo sapiens has been fascinated by the delights and pleasures of fermented beverages. The Chinese brewed an alcoholic beverage as far back as 7000 BCE, the Sumerians worshipped Geshtinanna, a wine goddess, around 2700 BCE, and in India sura, an alcoholic beverage distilled from rice, was a tipple of choice in the third millennium BCE.

Pleasurable as an alcoholic drink is, it is undeniable that the demon drink has ruined many a life, not only that of the toper but of their family and loved ones. And this provides fertile ground for the practitioner of quackery to ply their trade.

No I: Arthur Pointing and Antidipso

What would people give for a miracle cure that would transform even the most degenerate drunkard into a teetotalling paragon of virtue?

At the start of the twentieth century, Arthur Pointing (1868 – 1910) claimed to have just such a miracle cure, Antidipso, made from some previously unexploited herb from South America. His advertising, and the remedy was heavily promoted, was primarily focused on the fairer sex, the implicit assumption being that the drunkard was always likely to be a man.

"Drunkenness cured", the adverts screamed, "it is now within the reach of every woman to save the drunkard".

If you were worried about how to administer it, Arthur had figured that out. Poisoning seems to have been the most popular way for a woman to murder her victim in the 19th century. Slipping a phial of poison into a drink or dinner was the work of seconds and didn't require any brawn. This was clearly the way that a woman could trick her hubby into taking the miracle cure.

The adverts carefully gave the instructions, "Can be given in tea, coffee or food, thus absolutely and secretly curing the patient in a short time without his knowledge".

To get your hands on this wonder cure, all you had to do was to apply to Ward Chemical Co of Regent Street who, on return, would send a package of the remedy, securely sealed in a plain wrapper together with full directions on how to use it and testimonials galore. Packets retailed for ten shillings, worth it, perhaps, to get your hands on something which, according to the advertising copy, "has shed a radiance into thousands of hitherto desolate firesides" and which "does its work silently and surely that while the devoted wife, sister or daughter looks on, the drunkard is reclaimed even against his will and without his knowledge or co-operation".

But what was in it and did it work?

By January 1904, the *Lancet*, the medical journal, had Antidipso in its sights and published an analysis of its ingredients. They found that 78% of it was made of milk sugar and the balance, potassium bromide. There wasn't a hint of an exotic South American herb to be seen. Although bromide could make you feel sick and, possibly, put you off the demon drink, if only temporarily, the journal concluded that the quantities in a daily dose of Antidipso were so small as to be barely noticeable. What's more, the cost of the ingredients amounted to around one and half pennies. The retail price of ten shillings, even allowing for advertising expenses, showed a phenomenal mark up. No wonder within ten years of its launch, Pointing was worth almost £38,000.

Pointing tried to fight back, visiting the journal's offices and showed sheaths of glowing testimonials as to the efficacy of his cure. But to no avail. The *Lancet* savaged Pointing for perpetrating a "cruel and wicked fraud" on those who were trapped in a difficult situation by, in effect, selling them false hopes. But that, my friends, is what quackery is all about.

In 1906, Pointing had a mental breakdown and became a resident of Peckham House Asylum until his death four years later. He left part of his ill-gotten fortune to his employees and charities; perhaps he had found his conscience.

No 2: Quaff-aid

For the seasoned toper, a hangover is an occupational hazard. A real humdinger may provoke the resolution never to let a drop pass your lips ever again but, in my experience, these thoughts are even more short-lived than the resolutions we make at New Year.

Many of us have our tried and tested methods of dealing with a hangover, mine is to have a hair of the dog as quickly as I can, but wouldn't it be wonderful if you could pop a pill that inured you from the effects of a hangover?

Well, this is what Quaff-Aid purported to do. It was manufactured by Amber Laboratories in Milwaukee, a subsidiary of yeast processor, Milbew Inc, who were looking around for new uses for the by-products from the brewing process. The pills, made from concentrated brewer's yeast, were launched in the state of Wisconsin in the Spring of 1955. The adverts, as you might expect, were fulsome in their praise of the efficacy of the tablets.

"No regrets tomorrow for feeling good today", they screamed. They went on to promise "a wonderful time...every time. You'll be poised, assured, relaxed; have a wonderful sense of light-hearted freedom from worry because you know your fun won't be spoiled. Goodbye to hangovers!"

Not unsurprisingly, packets of Quaff-aid flew off the shelves of local pharmacists and bars.

For just ninety-eight cents you could get your hands on a Carry Home Party Pak, which consisted of five two-tablet packs. What's more the Party Pak came with some paper napkins and the helpful advice that a party hostess could hand the tablets out to her guests before the evening's festivities got into full swing.

I've been to a few parties where dubious looking tablets have been handed out, but never Quaff-aid. I'm not sure why you need a napkin to help you ingest a tablet, perhaps they were envisaging a crowd of drooling inebriates.

In October 1956, the Amber Laboratories in Buffum Street were visited by officials from the US Food and Drug Administration. They seized around a quarter of a million tablets, claiming that the product was no damn use. Perhaps one of the officers had had a skin-full and was rather disappointed, despite having summoned the assistance of Quaff-aid.

This prompted a furious response from the Director of Research at Amber, Sheldon Bernstein, who was reported by the *Milwaukee Journal* as saying that the vitamins to be found in Quaff-aid were essential for a speedy recovery from a bout of over-indulgence, but the FDA would not be moved and the product disappeared as quickly as it arrived and, doubtless, more speedily than a hangover.

Amber Laboratories, despite this setback, prospered, generating by the mid-1980s sales in excess of $10 million from manufacturing yeast extracts, animal feed supplements and distilling alcohol for industrial and domestic use. It was acquired by Universal Foods in 1983.

No 3: Hall's Wine

It is a strange thing, but for the late Victorians, nervous complaints were as endemic as allergies are for us today. For those who felt a little below par and were in need of a pick-me-up, there was a bewildering array of tonics. One such was Hall's Wine, which was introduced to the unsuspecting public in 1888 by Stephen Smith & Co of Bow in East London.

Another was Coca-cola but we will look at that gem when we meet John Pemberton.

Marketing is everything and Henry James Hall, the proprietor, hit on the wheeze of offering free tasting samples to anyone who bothered to write in. They were overwhelmed by the demand, so much so that they had to take out adverts in the press advising that "our offer... has brought us so many applications that our staff has been unable to attend to them on arrival. We are dealing with the letters in rotation, and hope to clear off arrears in less than a week".

I imagine the poor overworked staff had to glug copious amounts of the stuff to keep them going as they made strenuous efforts to reduce the backlog.

At its launch the potion, which sold at two shillings and three shillings and sixpence a time, was known as Hall's Coca Wine. Hall was perfectly upfront about it contents. "It is necessary to state", the same advert goes on, "that Hall's Coca Wine contains nothing but the extractive principles of the coca leaf and although a powerful nervine, is practically harmless".

So, dosing yourself up with cocaine is practically harmless, is it?

It turns out that there was more than just coca leaf in the Wine: Old High Douro and Priorato Port. I hope the bottle was passed to the left.

In 1897, the wine was rebranded, the Coca being dropped. It was not because Hall had any qualms about the cocaine content of his product, rather that he found that he was boosting the sales of inferior coca-based products. The adverts continued to boast about the efficacy of the tincture. It was ideal for when "you are neither one thing nor the other" and would allow you to regain "the last five or ten per cent of health, without which all is dullness". Hall even garnered some glowing testimonials from distinguished organs, such as the *Lancet* and the *British Medical Journal.* But trouble was looming.

Interestingly, it was not the cocaine that attracted opprobrium but the alcoholic content of the potion.

Teetotallers were fooled, so some temperance worthies claimed, into thinking that they were knocking back some medicated substance which, despite the name, didn't contain alcohol. For some, it was the start of the very slippery slope to alcoholism. The President of the Royal College of Physicians opined that "the prescription of medicated wines is in some cases responsible for the starting of the drink habit, especially in women" and one anonymous contributor thought "the devil in disguise is more dangerous than the devil with his fork and tail".

Eventually, of course, the cocaine content did for it, but it is a fascinating insight into the views of the time that the evils of the demon drink outweighed those of a variant of the Colombian marching powder.

There was a school of thought, though, that considered that less than enthusiastic abstainers saw the use of medicated wines as a way of getting their fix without overtly breaking their pledge. Whether the tonic did anything for the nerves is unclear, but it certainly took the market by storm.

KEEPING UP APPEARANCES

I N A SOCIETY where we are too ready to judge a book by its cover, the pressure is on the fairer sex to maintain or even improve their appearance by the application of cosmetics. Lamentable a commentary on society as this may be, it was ever thus, and the sale of cosmetics was always a tidy earner.

And where there is money, there is room for the opportunist.

Here are four examples of quacks who seized upon people's anxieties about their looks or how people perceived them in order to make a fortune. Inevitably, their products were not all that they seemed.

No 4: The Bloom of Ninon De L'Enclos

The first character in our story is the French authoress and courtesan, Anne de l'Enclos (1620 – 1705), who was given the nickname Ninon by her father. A noted wit and beauty, Ninon was said to have only used one cosmetic which "gave her the hue, the countenance, the vivacity and fire of youth, even at an advanced age". The recipe for this wondrous cosmetic came into the hands of a certain Mademoiselle Pigout who, in 1781, introduced it into England. It took off like wildfire, so much so that, according to contemporary reports, "its pre-eminent powers have now in the great and polite circles banished the use of every other composition that is set forth for the same or similar purposes".

Its powers were truly astonishing.

It would "cure effectually wrinkles arising from dissipation or old age, worms in the skin and pimples". By invigorating the blood vessels in the skin, the softened tissues took on a transparent and blooming appearance. On top of that, it was pleasing to the nose. At 4s 6d a bottle it was a tad expensive but, according to an advert from 1784, you might only need two or three bottles.

After cleansing the skin with oatmeal or Almond Washball and then drying it thoroughly, you were invited to pour a little of the fluid into a bowl, after shaking it well. Rub in well to the arms and face and, hey presto, it will "evince the pre-eminence of its virtues, beyond the possibility of a doubt".

So successful was the bloom that it attracted competitors

who punted an inferior product called the Veritable Bloom of the immortal Ninon de l'Enclos. Alarmed by these encroachments on to her profitable turf, Mme Pigout appointed "respectable agents in London to vend" her potion and to defend her patch.

So, what was in the potion and was it any good?

Well, according to an analysis conducted for the *Monthly Gazette of Health* in 1819, it consisted of white lead, almond emulsion and essence of lavender. White lead had been commonly used in cosmetics from time immemorial, usually mixed with vinegar to form what was known as ceruse. The problem with the regular application of ceruse was that women quickly became "withered and grey-headed, because this doth so mightily dry up the natural moisture of their flesh".

The *Monthly Gazette* was even more withering in its condemnation, citing the bloom as "of all the compositions that have been offered to the public, this is the most dangerous. The repeated application of lead to the skin of the face, instead of animating the countenance, would assuredly, by paralysing the nerves, render it inanimate. Such are the baneful effects of lead on the constitution, that the most serious consequences have followed even the partial use of a weak preparation".

It reckoned that the "cosmetic" cost a penny to produce, rendering a healthy profit to its manufacturer and purveyors.

Despite this damning report, it still appeared in the House of Commons' list of taxable medicines in 1830. Whether Ninon, who after all lived to the ripe old age of

84, actually used the stuff, never mind being solely reliant upon it, we can only conjecture. I suspect not.

No 5: Every Woman's Flesh Reducer

Obsession with body image isn't just a modern fad, and where there is a concern, there is an opportunity for the unscrupulous practitioner of quackery to operate. Today we are awash with diets, it is a multi-billion-dollar business, and it is hard to make sense of which one to adopt. Often it comes down to personal recommendation or how much effort the diet involves.

Wouldn't it be marvellous if the pounds fell off with the minimum of effort?

Well, that was the claim of the wonderfully named Every Woman's Flesh Reducer, manufactured in Chicago. It was, according to the adverts that plugged the product, an "easy, wonderful, external method for men and women". All you had to do was pour the reducer into your bath and step into the warm water. The results would be astonishing; "your superfluous fat will fade away, easily, surely and without any bad effects. Day by day your figure will become more and more as it should be – graceful, trim and beautiful". A marvellous piece of copywriting, if nothing else.

And that was it, no need to exert yourself, just sit back and relax.

"No need to starve yourself, dose with harmful, drastic drugs or go through exhausting and ridiculous exercises", the adverts advised. The Flesh Reducer sold for $1 or for an investment of $2 you would get three times the amount together with a money-back guarantee.

In the days when advertising standards were somewhat laxer than they are now, there was nothing like a bit of fat shaming to ram home the message, "you cannot be happy while you carry around with you that load of useless, energy-using fat. Rid yourself of the burden".

So, what was in the white powder and did it work?

The American Medical Association carried out a chemical analysis of the Reducer and published their findings in their *1914 Annual Report*. They found that it consisted of Epsom salts, alum, citric acid, camphor and sodium bicarbonate. Their conclusion was that "like every other bath salt sold as a cure for obesity, Every Woman's Flesh Reducer is a fraud."

An even more egregious example of fat shaming appeared in the adverts for Korein. "I Was a Tub of Fat", screamed the headline. These words were attributed to a Lillian Ianchuck who, before taking the red gelatine capsules that were Korein, weighed in at 190 lbs. After a course of the capsules she lost 40 lbs. "Now my weight is just right for my height", she claimed. "I have no more excess fat on me".

Other consumers testified to its efficacy. You could even send off for a free trial before committing to purchasing it. The adverts claimed that it consisted of bladderwrack, a seaweed which was popular at the turn of the 20th century as a weight loss supplement.

So, what was in it and was it any good?

Well, the Connecticut Agricultural Experiment Association carried out a full analysis in 1915. They discovered that it consisted of 40% sassafras oil and 60% petrolatum. Sassafras oil has subsequently been banned by the American Food and Drug Administration, because of its carcinogenic properties and because of its toxicity, it may have had some effect on people's digestive systems. The booklet that accompanied the capsules recommended a restrictive diet that may have helped but on the whole, it was probably best left alone.

Alas, weight loss requires some effort on your part, it would seem.

No 6: Edmund Lardner's Prepared Charcoal

It is salutary to remember that it was only in 1780 that Thomas Addis invented the forerunner of the modern toothbrush and that regular care of your teeth was hit and miss at the best of times. The desire to have strong, white teeth and the need to deal with any problems arising from the decay of your ivories provided the quack with fertile ground in which to operate.

A chemist, Edmund Lardner, sought to introduce a new tooth whitener to the great British public and by 1805 had produced a pamphlet extolling the use of his prepared charcoal solution.

According to his advertising puff, "it possesses the desirable qualities of rendering the teeth beautifully white; destroying the faetor arising from carious teeth, which contaminates the breath; removing the scurvy from the gums and stopping the progress of the decay of the teeth, while, at the same time, it is incapable of either chemically or mechanically injuring the enamel."

Students of the classics at the time would probably have noticed the rather uncanny resemblance to the verse quoted by Apuleius in section 6 of his *Apologia*, "I sent you, just as you asked me to, clean teeth and a bright smile, the product of Araby, a little powder, fine, noble and whitening, something to reduce the swelling of your little gums, to brush away yesterday's leftovers, so that nothing dingy and nasty might be seen should you part your lips in laughter."

Pliny, in his *Natural Histories*, reported that the regular usage of a tooth powder which included astringents such as myrrh, nitre and hartshorn, whitened the gnashers as well as strengthening the gums and assuaging toothache.

Lardner had by now rebranded his product as "superior prepared charcoal", to differentiate it from a rival version of the tooth powder bearing his name but sold by Alexander Blake, who had left his employ. It sold at two shillings and two shillings and nine pennies a box. A mouth solution was also available, retailing at 2s 9d and 5s 6d each. Prospective purchasers were warned to only buy the genuine article, bearing the signature of Edmund Lardner on the label.

The preparation was widely available at most vendors of genuine medicines. Lord Byron was a fan of Lardner's product and when he was in Venice in 1818, he asked Douglas Kinnaird to send him a supply.

What was in it and was it any good?

Well, the curious thing about Lardner's product was that there was precious little charcoal in it. The main constituent was powdered chalk, which was mixed either with a small amount of charcoal or with a pigment from the charred bones of animals. The concentrated solution was a distilled infusion of roses and myrrh – again revealing a fascinating similarity to the powders used by the Romans. It probably did work and activated charcoal is regarded today as a valid form of tooth whitener and neutraliser of odours. Black toothpaste is available in the Far East.

What brought upon Lardner the opprobrium of the medical establishment was his claim that charcoal was the principal ingredient. The *Medical Observer* commented sniffily, "in what respect roses and myrrh resemble charcoal, we know not" and the *London Medical and Surgical Spectator* objected to the misleading name, whilst being broadly supportive of the product.

A classical education can go a long way.

No 7: Dr Velpeau's Magnetic Love Powders

In cultures and times when arranged marriages were not the vogue, one of the principal concerns for the male was how to win over the fairer sex; and where there is insecurity, there is fertile ground for the practitioner of quackery to till.

Dr Velpeau – of course, that was not his real name, it was the more prosaic J C Merrill and may have been an attempt to associate his product with the French surgeon, Alfred Velpeau – offered his dupes powders which were supposed to transform their amatory fortunes.

What was most enterprising about the scam was that the adverts were in the form of a job advert for salesmen, offering a salary of 800 dollars and commission. When someone responded, all they received was a sample of the powders and some instructions as to their use.

"These powders" the literature proclaimed, "properly administered, are warranted irrespective of age, circumstances or personal appearance, to win them the love or unchanging affections of any one they may desire of the opposite sex."

The problem was in the proper administration of the powder. The male was not the one to take it. His task was to find a way to induce the object of his affections to take the powder. This might be an insuperable hurdle for someone who is particularly gauche in the presence of the opposite sex. Slipping some surreptitiously into a beverage might just work.

If he succeeded in getting the woman to consume the powder, the man would have an anxious wait to see whether she went weak at the knees and threw herself at him. Astonishingly, at the height of the scam in 1855, Velpeau was getting upwards of forty letters a day from men desperate enough to send him two dollars for the keys to unlock a woman's heart.

Perhaps unsurprisingly, nothing happened.

Many would put the failure down to experience, but some were incensed enough, in late 1855, to write to the Mayor of New York, complaining about Merrill's sharp practice.

The scam hit the newspapers but the victims didn't find a sympathetic press. One paper commented, "Only think of it! For two dollars, any enterprising young man — no matter if he is as poor as an editor, and as ugly as a baboon, can through the instrumentality of these powders, make himself "lord" of the most charming lass of "sweet sixteen" to be found within the limits of our friend's agency, which comprises four counties!"

The Mayor, though, proved to be more sympathetic and Merrill was arrested and charged with fraud. He eluded incarceration by promising to stop selling his powders and to return the monies extracted from his victims.

Whether he returned the victims' money is unclear, but the lure of easy money was too much to resist and six weeks later he was still at it, selling his miraculous powders and fleecing his victims. This time, though, Merrill couldn't evade the long arm of the law. He was arrested again, charged with defrauding his victims and thrown into jail. And that was the end of the Magnetic Love Powders.

Hidden Dangers

T HE ROMAN FABULIST, Phaedrus (c. 15 BCE – c. 50 CE), wrote, "things are not always what they seem; the first appearance deceives many; the intelligence of a few perceives what has been carefully hidden." This is an adage worth bearing in mind when surveying the practices of the quack.

Here are six examples that reveal some harmful and addictive substances lurking within a so-called cure for everyday maladies.

No 8: Angelo Mariani and John Pemberton

Cocaine, popularly known as Charlie or Colombian Marching Powder, is an illicit substance in many parts of the world these days but just over a century ago, some quacks were keen to market its medicinal properties.

The first half of our unholy duo is Angelo Mariani, a French chemist, who in the early 1860s was fascinated with coca and its effects. By 1863, he had come up with a drink which went by the name of Vin Mariani or to give it its full title, Vin Tonique Mariani (a la Coca du Perou). A mix of Bordeaux wine and coca leaves, the ethanol acted as an agent extracting the cocaine from the leaves.

It must have been a heady mix as it contained six milligrams of cocaine for every fluid ounce of wine. The colourful advertisements, often featuring girls dancing whilst sipping the red tincture from a glass, boasted that it would restore health, energy, strength and vitality.

It sold like hot cakes and the list of its users included the great and the good. Queen Victoria was partial to a drop as were the Popes, Leo XIII and Saint Pius X. Pope Leo even went so far as to award Mariani the Vatican gold medal and appeared on a poster endorsing the wine. The headline, Pope on Coke, clearly had a different impact in those more innocent times and was a boon to sales in Catholic countries.

Thomas Edison claimed, not unsurprisingly given the contents, that it helped him to stay awake longer and Ulysses S Grant found it useful in writing his memoirs, a sentiment anyone unfortunate enough to read them would readily understand.

In attempting to crack the export market, Mariani had to up the cocaine content to 7.2 milligrams a fluid ounce to compete with some of the cocaine-based drinks available in the United States.

This is where our other quack, former Confederate colonel John Pemberton, comes in.

Addicted to morphine used to assuage the pain from wounds sustained during the Civil War, Pemberton was keen to find an alternative to the opiate. Almost certainly inspired by Mariani's tincture, Pemberton developed his prototype drink, registered in 1885 as French Wine Coca Nerve Tonic, at the Eagle Drug and Chemical House in Columbus in Georgia.

Timing is everything, and in 1886, the state of Georgia passed prohibition legislation that, you might think, would have sounded the death-knell for Pemberton's drink. But think again. Pemberton simply removed the alcoholic content from his drink and relaunched it as Coca-cola. It was dispensed from soda fountains at five cents a glass and was marketed as a patent medicine.

The early advertisements proclaimed that it would cure, amongst other things, morphine addiction, dyspepsia, neurasthenia, headaches and impotence. Pemberton's potion cashed in on the belief in America that carbonated water was good for your health.

Coca-cola was heavily marketed. In 1888, tickets were printed and distributed, entitling the bearer to one glass of free Coca-cola at the fountain of any genuine dispenser of the drink. By 1913, 8.5 million of the tickets had been redeemed. The product was well on the road to global domination.

Coca-cola, of course, is now one of the world's leading carbonated drinks and it is fascinating to note that it owed its origins to a cocaine-based alcoholic drink, developed in France and promoted by the papacy. Today it is better known for its contribution to obesity and tooth decay and for its astonishing ability to clean jewellery.

But that is another story.

No 9: Morphina-cura Or Habitina

Sometime during the early part of the 19th century, Friedrich Wilhelm Serturner managed to isolate a yellowish-white crystalline compound from crude opium. After successfully experimenting with it as a form of pain relief, he called this new substance after the Greek god of sleep, morphine.

The development of the first hypodermic needle in 1853 meant for the first time it could be delivered directly into the blood stream and from that moment on, morphine became established as the analgesic of choice.

Unfortunately, of course, morphine was addictive; soldiers, like John Pemberton, who had been injured on the battlefield, were pumped full of morphine and their on-going dependence on the stuff was known as "Soldiers' Disease". Morphinism was viewed at the turn of the 20th century as such a scourge in polite society that it opened up an opportunity for unscrupulous quacks to exploit.

Step forward, Dr Robert Prewitt and Ryland C Bruce who, trading as the Delta Chemical Company, began in 1906 to promote Morphina-cura. Retailing at $2 a bottle, it was advertised as "an infallible remedy for the cure of Drug Habits of all kinds." Prepared for hypodermic or internal use, it was available through the post.

It was rebranded as Habitina in 1907, probably in response to the Pure Food and Drug Act which took a dim view to drugs being named in a way that suggested they were a cure for something.

Habitues, as the target audience of morphine addicts were quaintly named, were exhorted to "discontinue the use of all narcotic drugs and take sufficient Habitina to support the system without any of the old drug." The idea was that over time the addicts would reduce the amount they took until, eventually, they could live without it at all.

But, of course, life isn't like that and the unfortunate habitues swapped one form of addiction for another.

When, in 1912, Prewitt and Bruce were arrested and charged with sending poison through the mail, harrowing stories emerged of the devastation that their panacea had caused. One mechanic from Missouri had lost everything, consuming a $2 bottle a day and become a "maniac", a woman from Pennsylvania had lost her reason and went blind after taking Habitina, although she was eventually cured of her addiction in hospital, and, perhaps most tragic of all was a twenty-six-year-old woman who had spent more than $2,300 on the stuff over a five year period, even foregoing shoes to afford it.

Although initially convicted, it would appear that the duo were released on appeal.

What helped their case was that they were upfront in describing what was in their concoction, perhaps a side benefit of the tightening of legislation surrounding pharmaceuticals, even if it did not preclude the stuff being sent through the mail. The bottle's label had a skull and cross-bones in the top left-hand corner, beneath which was the legend "Poison". The label went on to announce that for every fluid ounce, there were sixteen grains of morphine sulphate and eight grains of a morphine derivative called diacytle morphine hydrochloride.

In other words, over the six years they were trading,

between 1906 and 1912, Prewitt and Bruce had made half a million dollars by supplying morphine addicts with a more expensive, branded version of the drug.

No wonder the habitues couldn't kick the habit.

No 10: Frank A Ruf And The Antikamnia Chemical Company

If nothing else, many of us aspire to a pain-free existence and where there is pain, there is an opportunity for exponents of quackery to exploit. The Antikamnia Chemical Company, the name is a cod-Greek word meaning opposed to pain, was founded in the late 1880s and registered in 1890 by a couple of drug store owners in St Louis, Missouri.

The little white tablets they produced were described in their adverts as "little short of an inspiration". Their five grain Antikamnia and Codeine tablets contained "4.5 grams of Antikamnia and 0.5 of a gram of Sulphate Codeine" and "one or two tablets [should be taken] every two or three hours or as indications may require." Users were given helpful instructions; "also advisable to administer with a little water, diluted whisky, wine or hot toddy."

And what was it supposed to cure?

The advert, naturally, gave the answer; "this combination is particularly useful in La Grippe, Influenza and all Grippal Conditions, Pneumonia, Bronchitis, Deep Seated Coughs, Neuroses of the Larynx etc, etc." It was also handy to be taken as a preventative before participating in sports or even going out shopping.

The medicine was never patented and wasn't a

prescription drug. Nevertheless, the company marketed it aggressively through direct mailing and promotional products to doctors in the hope that they would be persuaded to recommend it to their patients. In many ways, they were the forerunners of junk mail marketeers. Their objective was to get their name known to as wide an audience as possible and it worked. When Ruf died in 1923, his estate was worth more than $2 million.

One of the most bizarre promotional products that went out in Antikamnia's name was a series of limited edition calendars for the years 1897 through to 1901, produced by a St Louis chemist and part-time artist, Louis Crusius. They feature skeletons in a wide range of fantastic and comical poses and dressed, apart from a usually grinning skull, in everyday clothing.

To pick just three at random, one featured a newsboy dressed in rags hawking newspapers, another showed a skeleton wearing a top hat with a clover leaf, green sash and smoking a pipe and a third with a beer stein and the obligatory pipe. On the reverse of the calendar page was a description of the products available and the conditions which they were effective against.

These calendars routinely fetch a good price on e-bay and in antique shops.

Unfortunately, the tablets, which were based on a coal-tar derivative, Acetanilide, had a potentially lethal side-effect. They could cause cyanosis which as a result of a lack of oxygen could turn the taker's extremities blue. There were reports of deaths as a result of taking Antikamnia as early as 1891 and the *California State Journal of Medicine* in 1907 described a woman who had taken the pills as "practically without pulse, cyanosed, with shallow breathing and a leaky skin."

The passing of the Pure Food and Drug Act soon put an end to Ruf's business. In 1910, US officials seized a container of Antikamnia and prosecuted its manufacturers for not stating that the drug was an acetanilid derivative, a case that went all the way to the Supreme Court. Shortly afterwards, the company collapsed.

Leaving aside the dangerous and potentially lethal side-effects, Ruf may have been on to something. Half a century later, Julius Axelrod discovered that what acetanilide produces when metabolised is paracetamol, something we pop with gay abandon today.

So, Antikamnia may just have been effective as a pain-killer.

No 11: Perry Davis' Vegetable Pain Killer

In some ways, the tale of Perry Davis is an example of triumph over adversity.

Born in 1791 into a desperately poor family and apprenticed to a cordwainer, he was an inventor manqué, several of his patented ideas failing to attract investment and leaving him deeper in debt. He was also desperately unlucky. When fourteen, he fell off some scaffolding, breaking his hip, an injury that left him lame for the rest of his life. He suffered from respiratory problems, which the medics could not cure. Only two of his nine children survived. In 1840, he became very sick and was in great pain.

Eschewing medical practitioners, Davis relied on his own resources and started experimenting with a concoction of herbal and naturally grown ingredients. He had no high hopes as to its efficacy, rather anticipating it to be "handing me gently to the grave".

Miraculously, though, he got better only for ill fortune to dog him once more. After his house in Fall River was destroyed by fire in 1843 and he was on his uppers, he decided to concentrate on the one thing that had worked for him, his patent medicine. Even then, he had another setback. Whilst tinkering with the formula, a can of alcohol exploded, causing severe burns to his face. The application of his panacea did the trick.

If nothing else, Davis was a consummate salesman and imbued with absolute confidence in his product, he sold it for all he was worth. Bottles of the vegetable pain killer began to fly off the shelves, so much so that he opened a factory in the aptly named Providence.

Advertising was fulsome as to its powers. An example ran; "an inexpensive and thoroughly reliable safeguard is offered by Perry Davis' Pain Killer which…has stood unrivalled as a household companion. It is used externally as well as internally and is just what is needed for burns, bruises, cuts, sprains etc; and most people know that no other remedy is to be compared with it as a cure for coughs, colds, rheumatism, neuralgia etc. in winter and all summer complaints in their season…it is a medicine chest in itself."

Another featured a host of cherubs bearing the distinctive brown bottle.

Testimonials were cited, including one from Mark

Twain; "those who could run away did. Those who could not drenched themselves in cholera preventatives and my mother chose Perry Davis' Pain Killer for me."

Its fame spread overseas and during the American Civil War it was dispensed to soldiers and horses alike. An ardent Baptist, Davis gave bottles to missionaries to take with them abroad. His generosity was usually rewarded with a boost in sales.

As his personal fortune grew, he gave donations to many causes, gifting $50,000 in 1850 for the erection of a new Baptist church. When he died in 1862, his coffin was followed by crowds of the poor, whom he had helped. The production and sale of Davis' Pain Killer survived his death, his son taking over the responsibility and the potion was still on sale until the early 1940s.

So, what was in it and was it any good?

Although Davis never revealed the formula, it seemed that it was a mix of vegetable extracts, camphor, ethyl alcohol and opiates. With that lot inside you, it is no wonder you felt better, even if only temporarily.

No 12: Cordial Balm Of Gilead

Samuel Solomon was born around the 1760s in Dublin and moved to the north of England some time before 1800 where eventually he set up a patent medicine business in Liverpool. He styled himself as a doctor, but it is almost certain that what medical qualifications he may have possessed were bought rather than earned.

His most famous and successful remedy was this rather

grandiloquently named tincture which takes as its reference the balm of Gilead in the *Book of Jeremiah*; "is there no balm in Gilead, is there no physician there?" – nothing like a bit of biblical provenance to add to the authenticity of your products. From the 17th century onwards, balm of gilea had become synonymous with a universal cure-all in figurative speech.

Solomon was not shy in proclaiming the significant benefits to be had by taking the balm. It was said to have been distilled from liquid gold or to have been composed of the pure essence of virgin gold. In reality, it was little more than a mix of brandy and turpentine flavoured with various herbs. Mercifully, perhaps, there is no suggestion that it contained any of the opiates that were commonly found in contemporary potions.

Solomon's adverts focused on people's general anxieties and sense of hypochondria, easy meat in an age when medical knowledge was sketchy and access to what medical assistance was available was expensive.

To ensure that we recognised the true value of the balm, the adverts went overboard; "it offers the most invigorating powers. It warms and enlivens the heart, raises the spirits and promotes digestion, eases or cures nervous, hypochondriac, nervous and female complaints and lifts lassitude, debility and weakness arising from juvenile imprudences. So noble, safe and efficacious a remedy has never before been offered to mankind."

If you were worried about the taste, fear not.

"Besides the nutritious quality of a restorative, it has a fragrant, subtle, oleos principle, which immediately affects the nerves and gives a kind of friendly motion to the fluids, yielding plenty of animal heat, the true source of firmness and vigour."

Inevitably, access to this panacea came at a price with a small bottle retailing at ten shillings and sixpence and a large bottle at thirty-three shillings, astronomic sums at the time. Solomon even charged for the benefit of his expertise, as one advert makes clear; "Dr Solomon, when consulted, expects the usual fee of £1 to whom such letters, for safety, be addressed – Money Letter, Dr Solomon, Gilead-House, near Liverpool, paid double postage."

Yes, he named his grandiose house, built with the profits of his tincture, after his product.

He was famous for carrying an ostentatious cane with a large gold handle and for being somewhat careful with his pennies. When guests arrived at the house for dinner, they were provided with a bottle to taste. When it was time to leave, they were each presented with a bill for the balm!

Such behaviour seldom wins friends, though.

A group of men, whose wives were addicted to the balm, probably the alcoholic contents thereof, lured Solomon into a trap, forced him to drink a bottle of his own balm and then set about him. So shaken was Solomon that he left Liverpool, only returning again shortly before his death.

Solomon died in 1818 and with him went most of his business. Widespread advertising of the balm pretty much stopped in the early 1820s and although it appeared in the list for Stamp Duty in 1830, the Balm of Gilead passed slowly into the obscurity it deserved.

No 13: Dr Pierce's Favourite Prescription

One of America's greatest practitioners of the ignoble art of quackery was one Ray Vaughn Pierce (1840 – 1914), who operated from Buffalo in New York State. He was a prolific producer of panaceas for a whole range of medical conditions. But we have to start somewhere and where better, perhaps, than a cure targeted at the weaker sex. Indeed, the advertising for the so-called Favourite Prescription specifically referred to "weak women".

Pierce was not bashful in proclaiming the benefits of the Favourite, describing it as "a tonic nervine" which "quiets nervous irritation" and "strengthens the enfeebled nervous system, restoring it to healthful vigour". It was particularly helpful with women's problems; "in all diseases involving the female reproductive organs, with which there is usually associated an irritable condition of the nervous system, it is unsurpassed as a remedy."

There was more... It was a "uterine and general tonic of great excellence", naturally, and "an efficient remedy in cases requiring medicine to regulate the menstrual function." If that was not enough, Pierce topped it off with a further boast; "in all cases of debility, the Favourite Prescription tranquillises the nerves, tones up the organs, and increases their vigour, and strengthens the system."

As well as exhibiting the quack's natural tendency towards bombast, Pierce was also coy as to what was in this magic potion. The nearest he got was to suggest that it was "derived exclusively from the vegetable kingdom".

So that's all right then.

Perhaps more alarming was an advert in 1902, which was targeted at mothers, whose daughters were about to enter puberty. Naturally, Dr Pierce's Favourite Prescription could deal with everything that could beset a teenage girl but what was troubling was the final sentence; "there is no alcohol in Favourite Prescription and it is entirely free from opium."

Why did he feel it necessary to make this point?

It may well be because of a bit of a run in Pierce had with the *Ladies Home Journal.* The organ had the audacity to subject the potion to chemical analysis, claiming that it contained: savin, cinchona, agaric, cinnamon, water, acacia, sugar, digitalis, opium, oil star anise and alcohol. Pierce, by now a member of the House of Representatives, vigorously denied the claim and sued the Journal for $200,000, a case he won when a further analysis revealed the absence of opium and alcohol.

It is thought, though, that the crafty quack had simply omitted the offending ingredients between the time that initial article was published and the court case. It may be that the presence of opium and alcohol contributed to the potion's phenomenal success.

Pierce had form in using narcotics. His Golden Medical Discovery, which was advertised to give "men an appetite like a cowboy's and the digestion of an ostrich", the mind boggles, contained quinine, opium and alcohol. Even if these ingredients weren't ever-present, and a descendent who has Pierce's recipe book claims they were, there was a couple of troubling herbal ingredients. Acacia was known to dampen sexual appetite and response, while savin was known since Roman times to induce menstruation.

Dosed up with this, the daughter of the house would, unknowingly, be well protected against any advances from the lads of the neighbourhood.

Everyday Complaints

B EFORE WE BID a heart-felt farewell to the land
of quackery, we should look at a few so-called cures,
which had the commercial savvy to address a wide range
of everyday complaints.

You will probably have worked out by now that the keys
to success in quackery are to come up with something that
"cures" a multitude of complaints, advertise the bejeebers
out of it and sit back and wait for the money to roll in.

If you can extend the panacea's remit to include the
animal kingdom, so much the better. Credulity, gullibility
and desperation will do the rest.

No 14: Merchant's Gargling Oil

George W Merchant's Gargling Oil is a perfect example of the aforementioned rules for successful quackery and it served them in good stead for almost a century.

The liniment, launched on the unsuspecting American public in 1833, was intended to cure: burns, scalds, flesh wounds, a bad back, piles, tooth ache, sore throats, chilblains and chapped hands.

According to the adverts "Merchant's Gargling Oil is a diffusible stimulant and carminative", so you could use it to deal with flatulence. "It can be taken internally when such a remedy is indicated, and is a good substitute for pain killers, cordials and anodynes. For Cramps or Spasms of the Stomach, Colic, Asthma, or Internal Pain, the dose may be from fifteen to twenty drops, on sugar, or mixed with syrup in any convenient form, and repeated at intervals of three to six hours."

The first thing to note is that despite its name, it could be applied externally as well as internally. Secondly, it was marketed as being good for animals as well as Homo sapiens. Apparently, horses went mad for it.

Initially, there was just one version of the liniment but from the 1870s there were two distinct versions; a yellow tincture for animals and a lighter coloured liquid for humans. Even if you could only get your hands on the animal version, you could still use it. The adverts did warn, though, "it will stain and discolour the skin, but not permanently."

The Gargling Oil made extensive use of advertising.

As well as the standard newspaper adverts, there were almanacs, song books and stamps.

In the 1870s, Darwin's evolutionary theories and the suggestion that man descended from apes were causing waves. Disraeli noted, "Is man an ape or an angel? My Lord, I am on the side of the angels. I repudiate with indignation and abhorrence these new-fangled theories." The furore that Darwin's theories was causing was too good an opportunity for the copywriters for Merchant's Gargling Oil to miss and they ran a series of ads featuring an ape with the quatrain; "If I am Darwin's grandpapa/ It follows don't you see/ that what is good for man or beast/ is doubly good for me."

So, what was in it and was it any good?

The former is the easier question to answer as the adverts were unusually forthcoming. It was a mix of petroleum, soap, ammonia water, oil of amber, iodine tincture, benzene and water. It is hard to imagine what possessed Merchant to knock up this concoction but as it must have tasted awful, the instruction to take it with sugar would have been very welcome.

As to its efficacy, it is not clear. It would have been messy to apply, and the petroleum base may have been off-putting but it evaded the attentions of the American Food and Drug Association.

What did for it was a serious fire at the Merchant factory in Lockport in New York in 1928, which completely destroyed the building – I wonder if the Gargling Oil was flammable? – and it was so destructive that the company never got back on its feet again.

It did leave us, though, with some wonderful adverts.

No 15: Dr King's New Discovery For Consumption

Some diseases are still with us but over the course of time have changed their names. A major killer in the 19th century was consumption. We now know this wasting disease as tuberculosis and whilst there are antibiotics available, I still read of outbreaks in the press.

In the days before the vaccine had been discovered, the consumptive proved to be fair game for the practitioners of the art of quackery. One such was Herbert E Bucklen.

In around 1878, Bucklen purchased the rights to some patent medicines from a Dr Z. L. King and moved the business from Elkhart in Indiana to Chicago. The crown jewel in his Gladstone bag was King's rather prosaically named New Discovery, which was aimed specifically at consumptives.

Bucklen was a tireless advertiser, no journal was too big or small, and by 1885 he had established the New Discovery as a nationally recognised brand. His major coup came in 1893 when, at the Chicago World Fair, he offered for fifty cents a thirty-one page booklet, which contained colour lithographs of the world fair buildings together with extensive advertising for his products.

Naturally, the adverts were fulsome.

They proclaimed that the New Discovery was the only sure-fire cure for consumption in the world and that it struck terror in the medical profession, presumably because it showed their inadequacy in dealing with what was hitherto nigh on incurable. It was also efficacious, the ads went on, in dealing with "all diseases of the throat, chest and lungs and permanently cures coughs, asthma, bronchitis, incipient consumption, lung fever, pneumonia, loss of voice…" – the list goes on and on.

The copy becomes almost lyrical when it describes the perils of delay; "delay not a moment when that hacking cough and flushed cheek admonish you that the insidious viper, Consumption, is secretly gnawing at the vitals and, ere long, your doom will be sealed."

All the patient had to do was send off for a free sample and then further bottles would be available for just one dollar a time. The patient was warned to beware of all imitations and make sure that they only consumed the potion bearing Dr King's name.

The advertising worked, bottles flew off the shelves and Bucklen made a fortune.

The big questions, though, were; what was in it and did it work?

Well, what might fill honest medical practitioners with a degree of dread was that it was a mix of morphine and chloroform. For the consumptive, this was a pretty deadly concoction. The chloroform would supress the cough, a tick in the box there, but the problem was that it would suppress the natural reaction to try and clear the lungs of the stuff that was blocking them. Regular ingestion of morphine would induce a cheery disposition in the patient and the sense amongst relatives that the potion might be working.

So, a vicious circle would develop, hastening the patient's eventual demise.

Naturally, there was no warning as to the potential harm that regular doses of the New Discovery could cause, either in the advertising or on the label of the bottles. After all, the aim of the game was to maximise sales, not to look after the patient's welfare.

It took exposure from the likes of the *Journal of the American Medical Association* and Samuel Hopkins Adams in his book, the *Great American Fraud*, of which more anon, to bring Bucklen's money-making scam crashing down to earth.

No 16: John Hill And His Pectoral Balsam of Honey

John Hill (1714 – 1775), was a noted botanist in his time and a prolific writer, perhaps best known for his 26 volume *The Vegetable System*, its full title running to fifty-eight words almost required a volume in itself.

He was also a man of letters but was very disputatious and these vexatious traits earned him many an enemy. Samuel Johnson described him as "an ingenious man but [who] had no veracity" and the actor David Garrick wrote of him, "for physics and farces, his equal scarce there is;/ his farces are physic, his physic a farce is."

The Swedes, the race that is, not the vegetable, seemed to like him, awarding him a knighthood.

For a quack, Hill was unusual in that he had a medical degree and he put this and his botanical knowledge to good use to create a number of herbal-based remedies, including the pectoral balm of honey. He used the monies earned from his medicines to fund the publication of his books and earned a considerable fortune.

Honey has a long medicinal history, the ancient Egyptians using it for embalming bodies and dressing wounds as well as an offering to the gods. Holistic practitioners consider it to be one of nature's best all-round remedies but scientific claims for its efficacy remain unproven, save for the care of wounds and the suppression of coughs. When I have a tickle in my throat, I like to suck a honey-flavoured lozenge.

The trouble with honey as an ingredient, though, was that, in concentrated form, it was difficult to obtain in a sufficient quantity and at a reasonable cost to make a honey-based balsam commercially viable.

The actual base for Hill's balsam, according to the *Modern Domestic Medicine* of 1827, was an ounce of balsam of tolu (a South American resin which is still today used in cough syrups), a drachm of gum storax, fifteen grains of purified opium, four ounces of best honey and a pint of rectified spirit of wine. The brew was left to mix for five or six days and then strained.

Et voila.

As we have now grown accustomed to expect, the advertising that accompanied the balsam was effusive in its praises. "...the unequalled efficacy and safety of this elegant Medicine in the immediate relief and gradual cure of coughs, colds, sore throats, hoarseness, difficulty of breathing, catarrhs, asthma and consumptions."

To make up a dose you took a large tea-spoonful and mixed in a wine glass of water "converting the water into a most pleasant balsamic liquor, to be taken morning and evening." Bottles sold at 3s 6d and bore the signature H.Hill and were available from 150, Oxford Street and a couple of outlets in the City of London and one in Borough.

Whether it worked or not is unclear, but the mix of wine, opium, honey and tolu would not have been unpleasant to the taste, at least. But the principal ingredient of the balsam was tolu, not honey, as the *Medical Observer* of 1808 pointed out.

"The Balsam of Tolu, from its fragrant aromatic smell, is a ready and cheap substitute [for the cost and trouble of producing concentrated honey]. This deception was first begun by Sir John Hill who...did not lose sight of a balsam of honey which is nothing less than a balsam of tolu sold under this name. We regret that a man of Sir John Hill's abilities should have been put to such shifts."

Hill's ability to stir up a hornet's nest survived his death, but he did very nicely out of the sales, thank you very much.

No 17: Mother's Friend

I have never experienced it personally, but I have it on good authority that pregnancy and childbirth, whilst undoubtedly having its upsides, can be a painful and unpleasant experience. That being the case, I can understand why women might want to find ways to make the process of pregnancy and labour as comfortable as possible. So common is pregnancy, indeed, the survival of the human race depends upon it, that it offers an enormous opportunity for the unscrupulous proponents of quackery to exploit.

One company who seized the opportunity was the Bradfield Regulator Company, based in Atlanta, Georgia, who peddled a liniment called Mother's Friend for around thirty years in the States and Canada.

Selling at $1 a bottle, its virtues and properties were lauded in the advertisements placed in the press. One, dating from 1899, advised that it was for "expectant mothers to use externally. It softens the muscles and causes them to expand without discomfort. If used during most of the period of pregnancy, there will be no morning sickness, no rising breasts, no headache. When baby is born there will be little pain, no danger and labour would be short and easy."

Some of the adverts were almost lyrical in their proclamation of the liniment's amazing powers.

"To young mothers we offer not the stupor caused by chloroform with risk of death to you or your dearly loved and longed for baby but an agent which will if used as directed invariably alleviate in the most magical way the pains, horrors and risks of labour and often entirely do away with them..."

Others had a rather troubling eugenic twist to them. In an advert dating from around 1901, a Kentucky attorney-at-law is quoted as saying, "before the birth of my last one, my wife used four bottles of Mother's Friend. If you had the pictures of our children, you could see at a glance that the last one is healthiest, prettiest and finest-looking of them all."

An advert from 1902 went to great pains to satisfy the reader that there wasn't the faintest trace of opium, morphine and strychnine which many rival birth medicines contained.

That's a relief, then, but it raises the question: what was in the liniment and was it effective?

For many a quack, the Pure Food and Drugs Act (1906) began to make life a little difficult. With its extravagant claims, the Bradfield Regulator Company soon came under official scrutiny. On two occasions in 1909, consignments of Mother's Friend were seized and subjected to scientific analysis.

The good news was that, as the advert had stated, there wasn't a trace of a noxious drug amongst the ingredients. The bad news was that there wasn't really much to the much-vaunted liniment. The investigators found that it consisted of some oil, probably vegetable, and some soap. It was unlikely to cause harm but would barely alleviate the traumas of childbirth.

Mother's Friend continued to be sold but it went through what we would term today as a bit of rebranding and market repositioning. It was marketed as a massage oil designed to help with dry skin and the aches and pains of pregnancy. When the brand was acquired by the S.S.S Company, it became a body lotion and is still available today. As the website says; "keep all your skin smooth and supple before, during and after pregnancy with the creams that moms have used for generations".

The power of a placebo is a wondrous thing.

No 18: Hunt's Remedy – William E Clarke

Whatever happened to dropsy?

It first made its appearance in literature in Horace's *Odes (Carmina 2.2 13 – 16)* and was used by the poet as a metaphor for avarice. 18th and 19th century literature is peppered with references to people suffering from dropsy, but it seems to have gone out of fashion.

Perhaps that's because it is now known as oedema and is a condition whereby excess fluid accumulates below the surface of the skin, particularly in the legs and ankles, causing inflammation. What seems to cause it is an obstruction in the blood vessel, which once located, can be treated.

Anyone suffering from dropsy would be glad of some form of respite and a popular medicament in the second half of the 19th century was Hunt's Remedy. However, it was not just restricted to the cure of dropsy. According to the accompanying adverts, it was the "great Kidney Medicine that cures dropsy and all diseases of the kidney, bladder and urinary organs – never known to fail."

When the medicine came into the hands of a chemist from Providence, Rhode Island, William E Clarke, it was promoted, using some really wonderful trade cards. One showed a healthy male using a bottle of the said potion to wrestle a scythe-carrying skeleton. There was no doubting the message of this powerful image.

The adverts went on to say that "by the use of Hunt's Remedy the Stomach and Bowels will speedily regain their strength and the blood will be perfectly purified." In case you were concerned what was in it, the advert went on to reassure you that it "is purely vegetable and meets a want never before furnished to the public and the utmost reliance may be placed on it."

The potion came in two sizes: a small embossed bottle, known as Trial Size, retailing for seventy-five cents, and a larger one, which would set you back $1.25. The bottles were aqua-blue in colour. One of Clarke's agents, a Mr W B Blanding, sold 33,120 bottles over the course of two years and it was extremely popular throughout New England. But that was not the limit of its sales penetration. "The Remedy is known throughout the United States and Canada and in foreign countries", said the publicity material.

The story goes that the key ingredient of the potion was a root, which grew in the pastures and roadsides of the United States. It was used by the Dutch colonists for medicinal purposes. The recipe was eventually passed on to a number of physicians, one of whom used it to cure a Mr Hunt of Manhattan who, suffering from dropsy, took it for a year and saw that "his bloated flesh was reduced and his vigour restored."

Rather like Victor Kiam, he was so enamoured with the drug that he bought up the manufacturing rights and upon his death, these were acquired by William Clarke in 1872. The remedy was widely available until the turn of the 20th century when the 1906 Pure Food and Drugs Act put an end to its rather extravagant claims.

Whether it was effective was unclear.

Its main ingredient, according to the *Medical Record*

of 19th July 1884, was apocynum cannabium, or dogbane, which was used by Native American tribes to treat a wide variety of complaints such as rheumatism, coughs, pox, whooping cough, asthma and internal parasites. Whether it touched the kidneys or dropsy is unclear. However, the quality of the advertising images meant it has a special place in the annals of quackery.

No 19: Magic Foot Drafts

As old age approaches, the incidence of aches and pains, a bit of arthritis here and a touch of rheumatism there, blight my daily life. Stoically, I grin and bear it and usually the niggle will disappear as quickly as it came. For those who are afflicted with more prolonged bouts of rheumatism, the prospect of a panacea that will restore harmony to your body must be appealing. Naturally, there was a ready supply of quacks and chancers ready to prey on the gullible.

The Magic Foot Draft Company, operating from Jackson in Michigan, was actively promoting, in the early years of the 20th century, a cure for rheumatism in the feet.

Their modus operandi is now painfully familiar, extensive advertising extolling the benefits of their product and a money back guarantee. "Don't take medicine but try Magic Foot Drafts, the great Michigan external remedy which is curing thousands," the advert, featuring its corresponding secretary, Frederick Dyer, announced.

Reading on, whatever form of rheumatism, wherever situated "all yield quickly to those wonderful Drafts which have brought comfort to hundreds of thousands" – note the rapid increase in numbers from the headline – "including cases of thirty or forty years' standing" (or not, if you had trouble with your feet). "They are curing where doctors and baths and medicines fail."

What they were, these miraculous drafts, were plaster strips, made out of oilcloth and coated with pine-tar. They were applied to the soles of the feet, where they got to work and drew out the uric acid, or so the manufacturers claimed.

To avail yourself of these plasters, all you had to do was to send your name and address and you would receive a pair of drafts to the value of $1. If you were satisfied with the results, you simply had to "send us one dollar. If not, keep your money. We take your word and trust you for a square deal."

Presumably, they anticipated that most would persevere with the drafts and send for more with their all-important cheque. If you didn't communicate with the company, you were on their mailing list and they would soon follow up with a chaser. Some may have just then paid their dollar and put the whole thing down to experience.

For those who were not sure that the drafts were working, the follow-up letter would explain that complicated cases or the incorrect application of the plaster would not yield overnight results. Some chronic cases may require up to six applications.

The letter also warned against the patient becoming impatient or giving up too easily and just to reinforce the impression of its efficacy, would include glowing testimonials. The letter would end with a hint of menace,

"Unless you have already sent your order we shall expect a letter from you very soon, and there will be no failure to send the treatment just as you instruct, so you will have it and keep your recovery going steadily on day and night until every last twinge of pain has left you. "

Many would have paid their money for a quiet life.

And did they work?

According to Samuel Hopkins Adam in his 1905 expose of the patent medicine business entitled *the Great American Fraud*, "they [their feet] might as well be affixed to the barn door, so far as any uric acid extraction is concerned."

I guess not, then.

No 20: Ramey's Medicator

The nose is a good indicator that perhaps your mens sana is not in an entirely corpore sano.

Blocked, runny, congested, these are all signs that all is not well. Be that as it may, the nose has another attraction, it has two nostrils which allow access to your interior. Many of our medicines require us to inhale or apply drops but rarely recognise that we have two nostrils. Our latest purveyor of quackery, Alfred H Ramey, did though and his gloriously eccentric device enabled the patient to access all areas.

After sustaining devastating injuries, which resulted in him losing a leg during the American Civil War, Ramey settled down to run a market stall, selling medicines in Aurora, Illinois. Eventually, through hard work, he had a successful business. Why he decided to patent a do-it-yourself medical aid is unclear but on 3rd June 1890 he and his colleague, Frank D Rollins, filed a patent for their Medicator.

The design was fairly simple. There were three tubes, two which were inserted into the nostrils and one down the throat. An inner chamber contained wadding into which the medicine of choice – naturally, the Medicator came with its own Compound Inhalant – was poured. The vapours from the medicine would be blown up into the nostrils or down into the throat as required, clearing the head of catarrh and the lungs of phlegm. Four inches in size and nickel plated, with a hollow handle, which allowed you to store the instructions, and a cap for each tube, the Medicator came with four months' worth of compound inhalant and a tin of nasal ointment, all for ten shillings. Postage was free. The 1905 version featured a moveable mouthpiece for greater comfort.

One of its key selling points was that it didn't require any medical expertise to use and once you had bought it, it was always at hand. You didn't even need to use Ramey's compound inhalant.

Despite these obvious attractions, Ramey needed to advertise his product extensively and, as we have often observed with quacks, he was not shy in proclaiming its benefits.

"Cures catarrh, catarrhal deafness, headache, neuralgia, coughs, colds, bronchitis, asthma, hay fever and la grippe or your money refunded," an advert dating to 1895 proclaimed. "By the aid of this Medicator you are able to force highly medicated air directly to the seat of the disease, reaching even the remotest parts of the head, throat and lungs, cleansing them all of impurities, restoring lost taste and smell and purifying the breath."

"The Inhaler..." it goes on, "is without doubt far superior to any other remedy or device, as there is no irritating power or fluid applied to the diseased and inflamed membranes. On the contrary, nothing but pure and highly medicated air is used, which produces a soothing and cooling sensation to the parts affected, causing almost instant relief."

The advert does, however, attempt to dampen down expectations. "Please remember that chronic or deep seated catarrh cannot be cured in a day or a week but continued use ... according to directions... will effect a positive cure."

So, was it effective or was it just hot air?

It is difficult to tell but, suffice to say, Ramey did nicely out of it being "able to afford material assistance to many of his friends" until his death in 1923. Probably the Medicator, once bought, was the sort of thing that was put in a cupboard and quietly forgotten about.

Part Two

Financial Scams

Go West,
Young Man

THE WORLD TODAY is an incredibly small place.
With the resources of the Internet available to us,
global positioning systems and the like, we can explore and
examine any part of planet Earth from the comfort of our
armchair. But it wasn't always thus.

So small was the geographic circle in which most
people lived their lives that the tales of exotic lands,
boasting fabulous wealth, found a ready audience. And if
your daily existence was miserable, there was an enormous
incentive to pack your bags with what few possessions you
had and follow the advice of Horace Greeley to "go west,
young man".

Inevitably, though, the grass on the other side was not
always greener and scammers took advantage of people's

desperation and geographic ignorance to feather their own nest.

Here are three examples...

No 21: Gregor McGregor, the Cacique of Poyais

One of the most incredible fraudsters of the 19th century was naval veteran, Gregor McGregor, who, on his return to London in 1820, after fighting in the Venezuelan War of Independence, announced that he had been named Cacique or prince of the principality of Poyais. The honour had been bestowed on him, he claimed, by the native chief, King Augustus I.

And where was Poyais? According to McGregor, it was located on the Bay of Honduras.

To promote this land of milk and honey, he had a book published, ostensibly written by a Captain Thomas Strangeways, called *Sketch of the Mosquito Shore including the Territory of Poyais*. It told of a fantastic land with untapped gold and silver mines, fertile soil, an established civil service (always useful, I feel), a democratic government and natives who were eager to work for British masters. St Joseph, the capital, had been founded in 1730 by British settlers; strange that very few people had seemed to have heard of it.

Having piqued the nation's interest, McGregor rolled out his investment scheme. For the rich, on October 23rd 1822 he offered 2,000 bonds at £100 each, requiring a deposit of £80 and offering interest of 3%. They were fully subscribed.

For the poor, he sold land at three shillings and threepence an acre, about a day's pay. He even sold places in his military and positions in the government. Naturally, he devised and issued his own currency.

The Poysian Legation opened offices in London and Scotland and McGregor and his associates made hay, selling land, investments and other opportunities. So successful was the enterprise that by 1823 McGregor was, in today's terms, a multi-millionaire.

The problem was that this land of milk and honey didn't exist.

True enough, King Augustus did grant McGregor land in a drunken stupor but all it consisted of was four run-down buildings and uninhabitable jungle. There was not a sniff of gold or silver. But, as we know, facts never get in the way of a fraudster or a politician.

What would have been an elaborate and successful fraud had McGregor left it at that took a rather surprising turn when the Poysian legation, for reasons best known to itself, decided to send two boatloads of settlers to the non-existent land.

On 10th September 1822, the Honduras Packet left London with seventy settlers and on January 22nd 1823 the Kennersley Castle left Leith Harbour with almost 200 settlers. When they landed, the poor unfortunate migrants realised they had been conned.

Sadly, only fifty survived to return to England.

When the survivors made it to London, their story hit the newspapers and McGregor, sensing which way the wind was blowing, fled to France.

But McGregor wasn't done with his golden egg, that was Poyais, just yet and started selling investment opportunities to the French, repeating his trick of issuing bonds and making pockets of land available. The French authorities took less of a laissez-faire attitude than their British equivalents and started to investigate this racket, McGregor being arrested in December 1825.

Despite facing two trials he was acquitted but deciding that Paris was too hot for comfort, made his way back to England.

Incredibly, he was at it again, opening an office at 23, Threadneedle Street in London and trying to issue Poyais bonds in 1827, albeit with little success. In 1828, he was selling land in the mythical territory for five shillings an acre and during the 1830s, by which time he was now President of the Poyaisian Republic, he made several attempts to resuscitate interest in his fraudulent scheme.

Miraculously, though, he evaded justice and emigrated to Venezuela in 1839, where he died six years later.

No 22: John Law And The Mississippi Bubble

Fife born, John Law (1671 – 1729) was a bit of a rake.

Gifted with mathematical abilities, the son of a Scottish financier, he moved to London in his early twenties and made his mark as a gambler. When he was twenty-three, he fought a duel over a lady friend, killing his opponent, for which misdemeanour he served some time in jail. He managed to escape and spent a spell on the continent studying the financial systems of cities such as Amsterdam, Genoa and Venice, publishing a paper in 1705, in which he argued that paper currency should be adopted instead of gold and silver backed coins.

In 1715, the French economy was on the verge of collapse, the government defaulting on its debts and the value of its gold and silver-backed currency fluctuating wildly. Louis XV was only five at the time and control of the country's affairs was in the hands of a group of regents, led by the Duke of Orleans. Law was a friend of the Duke and saw an opportunity to put his economic theories into practice.

By 1716, Law had permission to open a national bank, Banque Generale, which, in return for deposits of gold and silver, issued paper bank notes. Although not legal tender, they were redeemable in French currency.

The bank was a success, building up its reserves from the issuance of stock and the profits gained from managing the French finances.

The French, at the time, had sizeable tracts of land in North America and in 1717 Law acquired the Compagnie d'Occident and, with it, monopoly trading and development rights for land under French control that stretched from Louisiana to Canada. In 1719, the Compagnie, now rebranded as Compagnie des Indes and with rights over all French trade outside of Europe, purchased permissions to mint coinage and to collect indirect and direct taxes.

Law effectively controlled France's finances and foreign trade.

Shares in the company were offered to the public

in January 1719 for 500 livres a time, payable in Banque Generale notes. Law had stoked up demand by promulgating stories – false, of course – of the untold wealth lying dormant in the territories.

It was too good an opportunity to miss and people from all social classes invested, making substantial paper profits – the French word millionaire was coined to describe someone who had made a substantial fortune through holding Compagnie shares – as the share price reached 10,000 livres at the end of the year.

Law's big problem, though, was that the bank had issued vast amounts of notes without the currency to back them up if anyone sought to cash them in, a problem compounded by the lack of gold and silver from the French territories in North America.

Inevitably, some tried to realise their profits by selling their shares, causing the prices to fall in early 1720. Law tried to avert a stampede by devaluing the share price by 50% and limiting payments in gold to 100 livres. This caused outrage and although the notes' value was restored, but not the pay-out limit, many investors now realised that the shares they had in the Compagnie were effectively worthless; paper millionaires were now real-time paupers.

By early 1721 shares were back to the original offer price.

Law, realising the game was up, fled dressed as a woman, and spent the rest of his life as an itinerant gambler. The bank and company collapsed, around the same time as the South Sea bubble came to its natural conclusion, and France was plunged into a severe economic depression.

No 23: William Playfair

Where there is desperation, there is always those who want to make a fast buck and to cash in on peddling false hopes.

The story of the Scioto Company is one such example.

The opening up of the west or, perhaps more accurately, the take-over of the lands of the Native Americans, meant that there were enormous tracts of land available for settlers.

The Scioto Company was founded by Colonel William Duer in 1727, its shareholders including Manasseh Cutler and Winthrop Sargent. It had arranged for the use of some four million acres of land north of the Ohio river and east of the Scioto river, on which the Ohio Company had secured an option from Congress. Congress required payment in six tranches before ownership of the land was transferred.

Of this tract of land, Scioto earmarked some three million acres for sale in Europe, particularly in France, which at the time was in the early throes of revolutionary fervour. Joel Barlow was appointed as European agent of Scioto and he teamed up with the inaptly named Englishman, William Playfair (1759 – 1823).

They formed the Compagnie de Scioto on 3rd August 1789 with some French investors, with the intention of buying land from the American Scioto company to sell to French investors in packets of 100 acres.

The plan was to use the money raised to pay Scioto, who in turn would pay the Ohio Company, who in turn would pay Congress, ample opportunity for monies to be siphoned off in the form of commissions along the way.

Eventually, the French investors would get the deeds to the land.

Playfair priced the land at six livres an acre but only required a down payment of 50%, the balance to be paid from the agricultural profits that the bountiful land would generate.

A contemporary, who had visited the site of the proposed settlement of Gallipolis, commented scathingly that Playfair's puffery didn't mention that "these fine forests were a preliminary obstacle to every sort of cultivation" nor that the nearest source of provisions was a year's travel away and that the natives were likely to be a bit uppity.

Playfair also failed to point out that what the French migrants were buying were merely pre-emption rights, not the land itself, as title to that remained with Congress until they had received the cash in full. But the desire to leave France and the promise of riches was such that Playfair sold some 100,000 acres around the Ohio river.

The problem was that he had not forwarded the monies to the American Scioto Company. So, when the first batch of 600 migrants arrived at Alexandria in May 1790, they were "disappointed" to find that they did not have title to the lands they thought they had bought. The reason was that monies had not been paid to Congress to secure it.

The Ohio Company arranged temporary accommodation for them over the winter and in the spring, the migrants set about cultivating what the brochures had claimed to be "the most salubrious, the most advantageous, the most fertile land known to any people in Europe".

Within two years they had almost starved and the

Scioto Company went bust, Duer spending some time in a debtors' prison. In 1795, the Ohio Company, which owned title to Gallipolis and the surrounding lands along the Ohio, magnanimously agreed to sell land to the settlers for $1.25 an acre, effectively requiring them to pay a second time for their land.

Playfair returned to England, after the revolution, and earned a living as a translator and essayist. He is also credited with inventing the pie chart.

Unmissable Business Opportunities

For the potential investor, there is nothing more exciting than being offered the opportunity to invest in and take a share of the profits from a business that is going to be a sure-fire winner. The wise investor should carry out some due-diligence before parting with their cash.

Not all did and here are five examples of unmissable business opportunities which weren't all they were cracked up to be.

No 24: The Gold Accumulator And The Electrolytic Marine Salts Company

If you could get rich by panning for gold from a river bed, surely you would get similar results, if you were able to explore the sea bed for the mineral? And how much easier would it be if you had a special contraption, the design of which was revealed to you in a heavenly vision, which could do all the hard work for you?

Such was the reasoning of the Reverend Prescott Ford Jernegan, a pastor in Middletown, Connecticut, who claimed, in 1896, to have the very thing to extract and exploit the gold residing at the bottom of the sea.

His contraption, called the Gold Accumulator, was hardly the epitome of the cutting-edge of white hot technology, consisting of a wooden box with holes cut into it through which the seawater would flow. The guts of the contraption consisted of a pan of mercury, containing a mystery ingredient, through which a wire ran to a small battery. You lowered the box into the water, left it overnight and when you raised it up again and got it on to terra firma, voila, there would be gold.

Jernegan interested a local jeweller, Arthur Ryan, in the box and Ryan decided to test it with a few of his friends.

To prove that there was nothing fishy about the contraption, other than, perhaps, some errant fish that strayed through the holes, Jernegan absented himself from the trials that were held in February 1897 just outside of Providence, Rhode Island. The trial proved successful.

When the Accumulator was hauled up, some gold flakes worth about $4.50 were found inside.

Although the amount of gold was negligible, the process was so simple that it could easily be expanded. There was little in the way of operating expenses, save the initial outlay for the Accumulator, and a thousand of the things, this is how many Jernegan reckoned could be built in a year, running every day would drag up a tidy amount of gold and provide a good profit, to boot.

Fired up with enthusiasm, Jernegan, Ryan and a few others established the Electrolytic Marine Salts Company, whose headquarters were in Boston but whose field operations were based in Lubec, Maine.

To begin with, all went swimmingly.

A handful of accumulators were generating $145 of gold a day and profits began to roll in. The company was floated on the stock market with an initial price of $33 a share. Within weeks, the share price hit the heady heights of $150.

But in July 1898 Jernegan, along with his unassuming assistant, Charles Fisher, disappeared and immediately the serried ranks of accumulators stopped bringing gold up from the depths of the ocean. The investors realised they had been the victim of an elaborate scam, the company folded, and they lost all of their money.

It seems that the secret ingredient in the mercury pan was Fisher, a trained diver. In the initial demonstration of the accumulator, Fisher had swum underwater, found the box and replaced the pan of mercury with one containing some traces of gold.

When the company was founded, and production was in full swing, the investors never troubled themselves to go down to Lubec. All Jernegan and Fisher had to do was present them with gold bars, representing the latest haul from the accumulators.

Of course, the bars were bought in Boston.

The directors' plans to expand the operations presented a logistical problem for the duo and so when they had made around $200,000 each, they fled, as all good fraudsters do, and were never caught. Perhaps filled with Christian remorse, Jernegan is said to have refunded $75,000 at a later date.

No 25: The Great Diamond Mine Scam

The California gold rush from 1848, and the Nevada silver rush of 1859, fuelled the idea that the mountains and riverbeds of the western part of the United States were stuffed full of minerals just waiting to be found. The idea of finding a source of untold wealth appealed to prospectors and financiers alike.

There was a ready audience for an audacious scam and where there is an opportunity someone will exploit it, as this tale involving two failed prospectors, Philip Arnold and John Slack, shows.

Arnold was working in 1870 in a San Francisco drill-making company, which used industrial-grade diamonds. By November of that year, he had acquired, or perhaps purloined, a bag of diamonds to which he added gems he had obtained from some Native Americans. He and Slack, the latter playing the taciturn foil to Arnold's more volatile character, set out to convince the great and the good of California that they had found a diamond mine and that here was the evidence.

The first investor the duo approached was George D Roberts, who was not only keen to get involved but soon spread the word around the principal financiers in the city.

In order to keep their potential investors sweet, Arnold and Slack offered to show them the site of the mine. The investors took up the offer and, accompanied by a mining engineer, they visited a remote spot in Wyoming where, lo and behold, the ground was sparkling with diamonds and other gems.

A sample of the stones was taken and sent to the great New York jeweller, Charles Tiffany, who affirmed their authenticity and placed a valuation of $150,000 on them.

The investors, who now included the likes of Baron Rothschild, Tiffany himself, General Dodge and George McLellan, were hooked, line and sinker, and persuaded the, doubtless reluctant, cousins to share their stake in the mine for $660,000 and formed their own mining company.

So how had the cousins fooled so many financiers so comprehensively in what *the San Francisco Chronicle* called, in 1872 when the truth was out, "the most gigantic and barefaced swindle of the age?"

Greed, of course, makes us blind and there was a bit of crowd psychology at play. If your peers are doing something, you don't want to miss out.

But the clever part of Arnold and Slack's scam was that they used real diamonds, firstly from Arnold's former employer, and then, when they had got some seed capital from the ever-obliging Roberts, they went to London and bought $20,000 of rough diamonds and rubies, a prodigious amount, from a London diamond merchant, Leopold Keller. Some would be used to show the size of the find to date and the rest would be put in the ground for the investors to "find".

This they duly did, the duo leading their mining engineer, Henry Janin, to an area laced with uncut diamonds. On the basis of this discovery, Janin wrote an optimistic report about the quantity of diamonds on the site, thus raising the stock price of the mining company further.

But trouble was afoot when the Government geologist, Clarence King, inspected the site.

He knew that the range and variety of stones and gems could not possibly have co-existed on the same site in the same geological conditions. He concluded that the site had been "salted", a term associated with tampering with ore to make it seem more valuable.

The land was worthless and the financiers lost their money.

The investors sued Arnold who settled out of court for around $150,000, still a tidy profit. Slack became an undertaker.

No 26: The Grand Central Information Booth Scam Of 1929

Sometimes, I stumble across stories that seem too good to be true and I bring this one to your attention with some trepidation, as the jury is out as to whether it really happened or not. However, the New York Central Railroad attested it in their brochure about the architectural wonder that is the Grand Central station in the late 1960s and, in the absence of anything to the contrary, that's good enough for me.

The marks in this scam were two Italian entrepreneurs, Tony and Nick Fortunato (or not so, as it turned out), who ran the Fortunato Fruit Company.

In early 1929, their premises were visited by a well-dressed man from the Grand Central Holding Corporation, called T Remington Grenfall. He had an astonishing proposition for them. The information booth that was in the centre of the hall was going to be closed down requiring travellers to get travel information from the ticket desks.

The reason for this change, he cited, was that too many members of the public were asking stupid questions and that the central position of the booth was disrupting the flow of people to the platforms.

What this meant was that there was an amazing piece of prime real estate available for rent to the first merchants, who recognised the gold mine that the opportunity was.

The Fortunatos fell for it, hook, line and sinker.

In order to secure the site, which was directly underneath the Golden Clock, the Fortunatos had to come up with a year's rent in advance, a cool $100,000. The following day, the brothers visited the Grand Central Holding Corporation offices, next door to the station, and handed over the money to the so-called president, one Wilson A Blodgett. In return they received a contract which stated that on 1st April 1929 (April Fools' Day, note) they were entitled to take possession of the space.

When 1st April arrived, the Fortunatos, accompanied by a number of workers carrying a large amount of timber, walked into the hall of the station to take possession of their spot, as per the contract. Imagine their surprise, when they saw that not only was the information booth still in situ but that it was manned and operating as normal.

The employees working in the booth refused to leave their posts and, worse still, the Fortunatos were requested to leave. Inevitably, the station denied all knowledge of any plan to rent out space in the hall and refused to honour the contract the increasingly frustrated Fortunatos waved in their faces.

It dawned on the Italians that they had been had and their next recourse was to go to the police. Despite an exhaustive search, neither hide nor hair of Messrs Grenfall and Blodgett was ever seen and the Fortunatos were forced to write off their loss to experience.

When something seems too good to be true, it generally is.

But Grand Central had not seen the last of the Fortunatos. Every now and again, they would return to the station and intimidate the poor folk working in the information booths and shout at railway officials. So notorious was their behaviour, that people would often go to the station on spec just to see whether the Italians would turn up and put on a show.

No 27: Victor Lustig And The Money Printing Machine

For the prospective fraudster, nirvana may well be the ability to print your own money whenever you want. Victor Lustig (1890 – 1947) went one further. He made his money by selling the prospect of being able to print your own money.

Born in Austria-Hungary but migrating eventually to the United States, Lustig had a long and successful career as a fraudster.

He even carried out a scam on the notorious American gangster, Al Capone, but had the good sense not to rip him off. He interested Scarface in an investment and took $50,000 from him. This he put in a deposit box for safe keeping. Two months later he went back to Capone and told him that the deal had fallen through but that he was able to return to him his investment.

The grateful gangster, impressed by Lustig's seeming integrity, handed him a tip of $5,000. Naturally, there was never any investment and what Lustig wanted to do was extract some money from the gangster without incurring his wrath.

His scheme worked perfectly.

Lustig spent part of his early career travelling the world on ocean-going liners. It was his opportunity to mix with the wealthy, improve his small-talk, he was fluent in several languages, and identify possible victims for a scam. When his mark had been identified, the conversation turned to the source of Lustig's wealth. With some reluctance and in the utmost confidence, Lustig would reveal that he used a money box, which enabled him to print as many notes as he wanted.

The mark was naturally intrigued and would beg Lustig for a demonstration.

Again, with a sigh and a show of reluctance, Lustig would shepherd the victim into his cabin and show them a mahogany trunk stuffed full with elaborate printing machinery. By way of a demonstration, Lustig would take a hundred-dollar bill and put it into the box. It would whirl away and eventually two perfect hundred-dollar bills would pop out.

The mark, now hooked, would be anxious to get their hands on the machine that could print their fortune. Money was no object and Lustig was able to command a price of up to $30,000 for a machine. Often, he had the luxury of two or more victims bidding against each other.

"There was only one problem", confessed Lustig. "The machine is very slow and takes six hours to print a bill". Sure enough, the machine whirred away and after twelve hours, just two more bills had been produced.

But the mark soon ran into a bigger problem.

Thereafter, the money-printing machine only spewed out blank pieces of paper.

Of course, sitting in the back of the machine had been three $100 bills and once they had been ejected, there was nothing left. By the time the mark had realised that they had been scammed, Lustig was long since gone; the sale was typically transacted at the end of the voyage, making this scam a classic example of where there is greed, there is someone keen to exploit it.

Lustig went on in the 1930s to become a major producer and supplier of counterfeit notes, until his career was ended by the jealousy of his mistress, Billie May. Thinking that he was having an affair, she made an anonymous call to the police, tipping them off about Lustig's activities.

He was arrested and although his briefcase only contained clothes, the police found a key in his wallet. This opened a locker in the subway station at Times Square where the detectives found hidden some $51,000 of counterfeit money and the engraving plates.

The day before his trial, Lustig escaped but was recaptured some twenty-seven days later in Pittsburgh. He was sentenced to twenty years in Alcatraz prison and died of pneumonia in 1947.

Lustig was a colourful character and the authorities couldn't quite come to terms with his profession and expertise. They recorded his occupation on his death certificate as an assistant salesman!

No 28: George C Parker And Brooklyn Bridge

There was a time when America welcomed migrants with open arms. Ellis Island and then New York was often their portal to a new life in the States. Many were innocents abroad and together with a steady influx of tourists, offered easy pickings to the unscrupulous. One such was George C Parker (1860 – 1936).

Those who live in or have visited the Big Apple will know that the Brooklyn Bridge, which spans the East River linking Manhattan with Brooklyn, is one of the iconic images of the city that never sleeps. With a span of 486.3 metres, it was the first steel-wire suspension bridge ever to be built, opening to the public in 1883.

On a whim, Parker decided to see whether he could sell the new bridge to an unsuspecting new arrival. And, surprisingly, he could and did, time after time. So successful was he that he concentrated on the scam on a full-time basis.

Parker would identify his victim in the street and sidle up to him. Whatever's happened to sidling? His opening gambit wasn't "psst, wanna buy a bridge?" Instead, he represented himself as the owner of the brand spanking-new bridge and was looking for a toll booth operator.

Was the victim interested? Bearing in mind they had often just stepped off the boat, the offer of immediate employment must have been attractive. If the victim showed a vestige of interest, Parker would then change tack. He would say that whilst he was a builder of structures, like the Brooklyn Bridge, he really couldn't be bothered with the hassle of taking the tolls.

Would the victim like, for a fee, to have exclusive rights to collecting the tolls from the steady stream of vehicles and pedestrians tramping across the structure?

This amazing offer seemed too good to be true, and, of course, it was, but many, unable to believe their luck and seeing this as a prime example of the land of opportunity in which they had just arrived, swallowed it hook, line and sinker.

There was no set price for the franchise. Parker just winged it and fleeced his victim for as much as he could. Some paid as little as $50 for the privilege, regrettably, a major proportion of their worldly wealth but, hey, it was a never to be repeated opportunity, whilst at least one person paid an astonishing $50,000. For those who found the capital outlay a bit of a stretch, Parker allowed them to pay on an instalment basis. Some paid for a number of months before they realised they had been had.

Of course, they would want to exercise their newly acquired rights and the New York Police were regularly called to the bridge to prevent Parker's victims from erecting a toll booth.

Emboldened, Parker turned his sales talents to selling other New York landmarks, including Madison Square Garden, the Metropolitan Museum of Art and Grant's Tomb. He also sold rights to successful Broadway shows and plays.

Eventually, the long arm of the law caught up with Parker and on the third occasion he appeared in front of the beak, in December 1928, after a career in fraud of some thirty-five years, he was sentenced to life in Sing Sing, where he died eight years later.

His misdemeanours were popularised in the expression for gullibility, "if you believe that, I've a bridge to sell you".

Now, that's what I call a scam.

Nothing New
Under The Sun

I T IS A mistake to think that financial crime is a relatively modern phenomenon.

Greed, after all, was one of the seven deadly sins, categorised along with gluttony and fornication as a lustful appetite. And where there is greed, there is always someone keen to exploit a situation to their advantage.

Here are two scams, variations of which are still practised today, which owe their origins to times long ago.

No 29: Zenothemis And Hegestratos

The entrepreneur is concerned with risk; to spot and exploit a gap in the market takes chutzpah and a certain amount of money. If you can use someone else's money along the way, that is even better.

Our next tale concerns a couple of likeable rogues, who may have perpetrated the world's first insurance scam.

I'm indebted to the Athenian orator, Demosthenes (384 - 322 BCE), for this insight into ancient financial skulduggery but it may be worth sounding a note of caution. Demosthenes was renowned for his oratorical skills and he was known to embellish his story to obtain maximum rhetorical effect. He was prosecuting Zenosthemis and so would have been keen to put the merchant in the worst possible light. We don't have Zenosthemis' side of the story and Hegestratos didn't live to tell the tale.

But the case did trouble the Attic courts and so we have to assume that there is a nugget of truth in the orator's account of the escapade.

Maritime trade was a risky business.

The principal risks were that the ship would capsize, and the goods sink to the bottom of the sea or that the ship would be boarded by pirates. Often the merchants would take the financial risks associated with the venture themselves, funding the journey and reaping all of the rewards. But more often, during the second half of the 4th century BCE, the merchants would seek passive investors, who would fund some or all of the venture, receiving as their reward a cut of the profits once the voyage had been completed. The downside of the deal was that if the vessel sank or was hijacked, the investors would lose their money, an early form of what we now know as bottomry.

Our shady duo cooked up a scheme which would rely on the rules of bottomry.

The plan was fairly simple. They raised the money necessary to fill their ship up with corn from innocent investors. But instead of buying the corn, they would pocket the monies and send it to their home town of Massalia, now modern-day Marseilles.

All they had to do was to sail the empty ship away from Athens and some way out at sea, scuttle it, making good their escape by means of a small boat they were towing behind. The crew may have gone down to Davy Jones' locker but, under the terms of the contract, Zenothemis and Hegestratos would get to keep all of the money.

So the empty boat set out with some passengers and when it was some two or three days out at sea, Hegestratos went down to the hold. Zenothemis stayed on the deck with the passengers, pretending to be unaware of what was afoot.

Hegestratos proceeded to cut away the bottom of the boat but the noise he made roused suspicion. Members of the crew and some of the passengers went down to the hold and caught the fraudster red-handed. Realising that the game was up, Hegestratos made good his escape, jumping overboard, but as it was dark, he missed the rescue boat and drowned, suffering the fate that he had intended for the innocent passengers and crew.

Zenothemis was arrested as details of the fraud were revealed and was left to face the Athenian courts and the rhetorical mastery of Demosthenes.

The prospect of making a few bob by skulduggery has been irresistible since age immemorial, it would seem.

No 30: The Letters Of Jerusalem

Occasionally, just very occasionally, I get an unsolicited email pop into my in-box, usually from an African unknown to me, telling me that they have access to untold wealth. If I would only send them a small sum of money and my bank account details, then they will transfer the money to me, I can take my slice and everything in the garden will be rosy. Smelling a rat, I have never been tempted but the sheer frequency of these emails suggests that some must take the bait, lured by the prospect of getting rich quick.

It seems that these emails, which are known as advance fee fraud, follow a long, if ignoble, tradition, dating back to at least the late 18th century and revolutionary France, if an account published in his memoirs by Eugene Francois Vidocq is to be believed.

Vidocq was an interesting character, having been an accomplished thief, who then became a policeman. When he retired from the force in 1827, he had amassed a fortune of half a million francs. He was also the model for Jacques Collin in Balzac's *Pere Goriot*, but that is by the by.

The scam was conducted by prisoners and guards at the Bicetre prison which was in a southern suburb of Paris. The starting point was to compile a list of the rich living in the targeted area, particularly those with anti-revolutionary sentiments. The scammers would then compose what they termed a letter of Jerusalem. Vidocq gave an extensive version of the type of letter, containing many of the characteristics of the modern scamming email, which I will abridge for convenience.

It would start off, "you will doubtlessly be astonished at receiving a letter from a person unknown to you who is about to ask a favour from you; but from the sad condition in which I am placed, I am lost if some honourable person will not lend me succour". The correspondent then went on to spin a tale in which he and his master were emigrating from revolutionary France, on foot to avoid suspicion, with a casket containing "sixteen hundred francs in gold and the diamonds of the late marchioness". They were beset by assailants and the valet, acting on his master's orders, threw the casket into a ditch.

Once the party had reached their foreign destination, funds began to run low and so the valet was sent back to France to recover the casket. The valet was about to recover the casket from the ditch when further troubles befell him. "I prepared to fulfil my mission, when the landlord ... a bitter Jacobin, remarking my embarrassment when he proposed to drink the health of the republic" – a phrase designed to further win the support of the recipients –"had me apprehended as a suspected person".

He was now languishing in jail and if the recipient could only find it in his heart to send some money, then the casket would be recovered, and the profits split.

Vidocq claimed that 20% of the letters elicited a response, with some correspondents even offering to recover the casket from its hiding place.

Often a batch of letters would raise the not inconsiderable sum of between 12 and 15,000 francs. Some even visited the area in the hope of finding the casket without the aid of their correspondent but, needless to say, their searches turned up nothing.

One cloth seller, from the Rue de Prouvaires, was caught undermining one of the arches of the Pont Neuf in Paris in an attempt to find the diamonds of the Duchess de Bouillon, which is where his correspondent claimed to have hidden them.

It just goes to show, there is nothing new under the sun.

COOKING THE BOOKS

I STARTED MY working career as an audit assistant, employed by one of the major London accounting firms. Supplied with a fistful of crayons, I was deployed to work my way through and reconcile various large and dusty ledgers, putting ticks on figures that balanced. I amused myself by humming the line from Pink Floyd's *Time,* "ticking away the hours that make up a dull day", and quickly realised that a career of double-entry book keeping was not for me.

Still, during my brief sojourn in the world of accountancy, I was taught to look out for the classic signs of accounting skulduggery, some of which are to be found in the following examples.

No 31: John Sadlier

Charles Dickens' Mr Merdle (*Little Dorrit*) and Anthony Trollope's Augustus Melmotte (*The Way We Live Now*) are larger than life literary characters, the epitome of all that was wrong with the Victorian capitalist system. There is little doubt that these characters were based on John Sadlier (1813 – 1881), an Irish financier and Member of Parliament, dubbed by the contemporary press as the Prince of Swindlers, when his peculations were unearthed.

Although he started his working career as a solicitor in Dublin, he founded the Tipperary Joint Stock bank with his uncle, James Scully, in 1838, offering above average interest rates to small farmers and tradesmen. The bank prospered.

In 1847 Sadlier was elected Member of Parliament for Carlow. On moving to London to take up his seat, he was appointed chairman of the London County Joint Stock Banking Company the following year. It was from this base that he began his investment career, financing railway developments in Sweden, France and Italy, founding his own Dublin newspaper, the *Weekly Telegraph* and buying swathes of land, valued at over £250 million.

Sadlier seemed to have the Midas touch and quickly became a household name as the Warren Buffett of his era. He couldn't fail and returned dividends of 6%, significantly higher than his competitors, to his delighted shareholders.

In parliament, he led what was known as the Pope's Brass Band, a group of MPs who resisted the Liberal government's attempt to restructure the Catholic Church, founded the Catholic Defence Association and in late 1852 became Junior Lord of the Treasury.

But like Midas, he was doomed.

Not everything was as it seemed. The high dividends were only payable because of fraudulent book-keeping and over-valuation of the companies' assets. In 1853, Sadlier was forced to resign his parliamentary seat when an investigation into his election campaign of 1852 showed that the financier had used his bank to bring pressure to bear on 208 voters in the Carlow constituency.

Sadlier started to make increasingly reckless investments, borrowing heavily from his own bank, forging shares in the Royal Swedish Railway Company, of which he was chairman, and rather desperately and unsuccessfully sought the hand of any Catholic heiress with enough money to get him out of his difficulties.

By February 13th, 1856 the writing was on the wall.

The London agents of the Tipperary Bank refused to cash drafts that Sadlier sent them. The following weekend he wrote a despairing letter to a cousin in which he confessed to "numberless crimes of a diabolical nature" causing "ruin and misery and disgrace to thousands – ay, tens of thousands."

On the night of February 16[th,] he went to Hampstead heath and, behind Jack Straw's Castle, took prussic acid from a silver cream jug, Melmotte's chosen form of suicide, and was found the next day.

Sadlier may have escaped justice but his peculations left many ruined. His overdraft was £250,000 and his collapsed banking empire owed the Bank of Ireland £122,000. He had defrauded the Royal Swedish Railway Company to the tune of £300,000. Over £400,000 was lost by depositors, an enormous sum given that the total deposits of all the joint stock banks in Ireland at the time was £12 million.

Sadlier's brother, James, an MP at the time, had also put his hand in the till and upon his brother's death fled, ultimately to Paris, where he was spotted and ordered to return to Westminster. He refused to attend and was expelled, the first MP to suffer this fate in half a century. James eventually settled in Zurich and in June 1881, he was set upon by a knife-wielding man who stabbed him to death.

Maybe the assassin was a creditor with a long memory.

No 32: George Hudson And The Railway Mania

The railways transformed the economic fortunes of England in the 19th century.

The nascent railway industry provided the perfect opportunity for the unscrupulous to make hay. Although a Private Members' bill was required to pass through parliament to authorise any new railway company as a measure to prevent fraud and the presentation of unviable proposals, this did not prevent the "entrepreneurs" spending all their investors' money before the bill reached parliament; as happened with the West End and Southern Counties railway, the Bristol and Liverpool line and the Northampton, Bedford and Cambridge line.

If a bill made it to parliament, there were significant

conflicts of interest at play. Many MPs were substantial investors in the proposed schemes and so would naturally vote them through. Other MPs were paid in guineas, the origin of the phrase guinea pig, by scheme proponents to lend their support to the cause. Newspapers puffed the advantages of a railway line and the development of a modern stock exchange made it easy for members of the public to invest.

Often shares could be purchased for as little as a 10% deposit with the railway company retaining the right to call the balance at any time. Many small investors, lured by the promise of significant dividends to be earned from fool-proof schemes, sunk their savings into buying railway shares, even those who could barely afford the deposit.

The problems came when the train wheels met the tracks. It soon became apparent that many of the railways were not as easy to construct as their proponents had claimed and even when operational, the profits to be had were not as great as were originally anticipated.

In late 1845, the Bank of England increased interest rates, which led to share prices in railways levelling out and then plummeting. Investment stopped almost overnight, leaving companies without funding and investors without the prospect of any return on their investments.

This mayhem gave George Hudson (1800 – 1871) his opportunity.

The larger railway companies, such as the Great Western and Hudson's Midland, bought up some of the failing lines for a fraction of their value, offering shareholders a below par value for their shares. Even so, many middle-class families had lost everything when the bubble eventually burst.

On getting his hands on a railway company, Hudson's modus operandi was to cut costs, often at the expense of safety, offer significant dividends to investors and to cook the books.

A pamphlet called "*The bubble of the age*", published in 1848, accused Hudson of paying dividends out of capital rather than revenue. Whether this was actually true or not cannot be conclusively proven, but what is clear is that the finances of Hudson's companies were built on sand. He had borrowed £400,000 at a high interest rate, which had to be paid back in 1849.

The vultures were beginning to circle and his shareholders were furious.

It soon emerged that Hudson had been selling shares between his companies at exorbitant values, when rumbled he had to pay back £30,000, and had used the monies of the York and North Midland railway (YNMR) to build a private station at Londesborough Park, where he happened to live. Faced with demands to repay £750,000, Hudson sold his home (and possibly the station) and repaid £200,000.

In 1852, the YNMR magnanimously agreed to release Hudson from all his remaining liabilities for £50,000.

Foolishly, Hudson rejected the offer and the matter went to court. He lost the court case and, in the winter of 1853, had to negotiate a settlement of £72,670 to clear his debts. His property at Newby Park went under the auctioneer's hammer.

Small consolation, perhaps, for the many who had bought a ticket to nowhere.

No 33: George Haworth And The Savings Banks

We are all encouraged to put a little by for a rainy day. Indeed, governments have sometimes taken a proactive role in embedding the instinct to save in its citizens.

In 1817, the then British government passed an Act, empowering the National Debt Commissioners to pay 4% interest on all sums deposited with them by savings banks. Even though the amount of interest offered was gradually reduced and the maximum amount you could deposit capped, by the 1840s, there were around 500 government savings banks, serving one million depositors and boasting combined assets of some £30m.

One such was the Rochdale Savings Bank.

The actuary and manager of this institution was one George Haworth, a Quaker and former cotton master, who was known for his "uprightness and strict integrity." His generosity made him a popular figure amongst employees and others. He had been in post for 20 years, claiming that he devoted his time "as a matter of charity".

Although the 1817 Act intended funds deposited with savings banks to be invested in government securities, in practice the managers had sole discretion as to how to use the money.

This is where Haworth saw his opportunity.

Haworth set up two sets of books, one of which was

for public consumption and the other, a cash book and a private ledger. In the latter, he detailed the thousands of deposits which he had diverted for his own purposes rather than those of the bank.

But the one thing that a successful swindler is not is immortal.

In 1849, when Haworth left this mortal coil, the trustees, who must have been asleep at the wheel, discovered that there were "deficiencies" of around £71,000, about three-quarters of the bank's total deposits. The embezzlement had been going on for some ten years or so.

Not all was lost. Haworth's estate yielded £16,000 and the trustees subscribed £17,000 in conscience money, but depositors were still out of pocket to the tune of £38,000. Of those affected by Haworth's peculations were 1,014 women, 539 labouring men, 191 sick clubs and 1,184 under the age of twenty-one.

Such was the size of Haworth's embezzlement that it made front page news and the government of the day launched an investigation into the affairs of all of the savings banks.

Reporting in 1852, the investigators revealed that some £160,000 had been "lost" at eighteen banks between 1845 and 1851. The report also revealed an astonishing level of laxity amongst trustees, who rarely, if ever, supervised the executive of the banks.

Even returns to the National Debt Office were full of holes, the ledgers of Cuffe Street Bank revealed 320 deposits of between £100 and £150 whereas the official return showed deposits of some £13,173!

Those who were rumbled included John Johnson, a wealthy colliery owner, who had got away with over £10,000 from the St Helen's Savings Bank, Thomas Smurwaite, a well-respected wine merchant, who salted £3,000 away from the Scarborough Savings Bank, and David Jardine, a draper, who embezzled £2,000 from the Dartford Savings Club.

In pretty much all of the cases, the embezzler had followed Haworth's simple but effective ruse of keeping two sets of books and relying on the doziness of their bank's trustees.

No 34: Jabez Balfour And The Liberator Building Society

The wonderfully and, as it turned out, appropriately named Jabez Balfour (1843 – 1916) is probably one of the greatest fraudsters in British financial history.

His first name, it is Hebrew for one who causes pain and sorrow, was a popular moniker until its lustre was inevitably tarnished by its association with Balfour.

Ostensibly a pillar of society (he was a member of parliament for Tamworth (1880 – 1885) and Burnley (1889 – 1893) and the first mayor of Croydon), Jabez made his mark in financial circles by encouraging the working man to save hard and buy his own home.

The Liberator Building Society, of which Balfour became managing director at the age of thirty-seven, was positioned to improve the fortunes of the down-trodden. Prominent non-conformist ministers were appointed to the Board to give it respectability and to encourage their flocks to invest. Profits, Jabez claimed, would go towards funding house building and improving living conditions of the poor.

By 1888, the Society had amassed assets of some £750,000 and whilst some of the monies were used to fund good works, most of it funded the purchase of properties owned by Balfour at exorbitant prices or to fund wildly speculative projects. One such scheme was to turn mudflats in the Isle of Wight into an upmarket seaside resort.

The final decade of the 19th century saw a downturn in the economy, severely hitting speculative ventures, in turn causing investors to look more closely at where they had placed their monies. The press, especially the *Economist* and the *Financial Times*, took a particular interest in the fortunes of the Liberator.

Their investigations revealed that the society, together with its connected companies, mainly traded with each other and overvalued assets were assigned to whichever company was about to announce its trading results, to exaggerate the strength of balance sheets and increase the dividends payable. The companies' auditors were often impoverished non-Conformist ministers who, glad of a few bob, signed the accounts off on the nod.

Balfour's own auditor was his tailor!

Balfour might have got away with his fraud had economic conditions not deteriorated. In 1892, rumours swept the City that the Liberator was in trouble and in October, it was forced to shut its doors, leaving at least 25,000 depositors ruined.

Half were over sixty years of age with limited means. A seventy-year-old spinster from Hertfordshire went mad and a bookseller in Peckham, who must have been a contortionist, is reputed to have cut off his own head. Several directors were arrested but Balfour, like all good fraudsters, escaped – to Argentina.

Thanks to the perseverance of Inspector Frank Froest of Scotland Yard, Balfour was kidnapped, after thirteen months on the run, and returned to England to stand trial.

Sentencing him to fourteen years in November 1895, he served eleven, the judge said "No prison doors can shut from your ears the cry of the widow and orphan whom you have ruined".

The Economist was more sententious; "to the worldly-wise, the mixing up of religion and business and the public appeals for Divine guidance in company matters, are regarded ..as marks of the Pharisee and as danger signals which it would be unwise to ignore. Balfour's conduct would have been bad enough under any circumstances, but the hypocrisy which permeated it from beginning to end made it infinitely more contemptible than if he had been an ordinary financial scoundrel".

Balfour wrote a best-seller, *My Prison Life*, upon release and in August 1915, at the age of seventy-one, went to work in a tin mine in Mandalay. He was sent home, the manager fearing the heat would kill him, and he died of a heart attack on the London to Fishguard train six months later en route to another mining job.

No 35: Alexander Fordyce

One of the reasons always cited for the Bostonians getting a bit uppity and for Britain losing the thirteen colonies, was the introduction of the Tea Act, with its infamous levy on our national drink.

If that is the case, then much of the opprobrium can be heaped upon the head of Alexander Fordyce, a stock jobber and partner in Neal, James, Fordyce and Neal.

Alexander was no stranger to the riches that can be untapped from a successful career in what we now know as the financial services. He made a fortune, having gained early intelligence on the signing of the preliminaries to the peace of Paris in 1763 and on the substantial increase in stock prices in the East India Company in 1764-5.

He was wealthy enough to build a stately home in leafy Surrey in Roehampton and an estate in Scotland, the land of his birth. He ran, unsuccessfully, for parliament for the borough of Colchester, spending £14,000 on his campaign, only to lose by twenty-four votes.

But it was the East India Company that proved to be his undoing. He gambled astronomical sums on the expectation that the price of shares in the company would take a tumble, something that didn't happen. Rather like an eighteenth-century Nick Leeson he chased his losses, using the funds of his depositors to cover his losses.

But a disastrous end for all was inevitable.

On 9th June 1772, Fordyce returned home with a wild, deranged look in his eyes, shouting "I always told the wary ones and the wise ones, with heads of a chicken and claws of a corbie (Scottish dialect for a crow) that I would be a man or a mouse: and this night, this very night the die is cast, and I am… am… a man. Bring champagne. And butler, Burgundy below! Let tonight live for ever. Alexander is a man".

The next day, hopefully, with a hangover, he fled to France, leaving others to clear up the mess he had caused.

And it was quite a mess.

The bank had to close and two days later, three other London banking firms with Scottish connections collapsed. By the 21st June twenty two banks, some of the larger banks and many smaller ones, had stopped making payments, never to resume trading. The Government forced the Bank of England to intervene and provide the London-based banks with sufficient cash to weather the economic difficulties, but those banks north of the border were not so lucky.

The Scottish banks, especially those in Edinburgh, had been borrowing from the Ayr Bank, also known as Douglas, Heron & Co, one of the twenty-two to bite the dust, partly to fund the development of the New Town area in the capital. The financial stability of Scotland was seriously undermined, and many public amusements and theatrical performances were cancelled, as the acting fraternity had invested heavily in Fordyce's ventures. The architect, John Adams and his brothers, engaged in the development of the Adelphi Theatre in London, were so strapped for cash that they had to lay off 2,000 workers. The contagion spread to Amsterdam, where only the formation of a co-operative fund steadied the financial system.

Ironically, the financial crisis so weakened the East India Company that they lobbied the government to pass the Tea Act.

And we all know what happened next.

As for Fordyce, he returned to England in September 1772 with debts of around £100,000 hanging around his neck. But he was irrepressible, standing again for parliament for Colchester where he was once more unsuccessful. He died in 1789, his demise described in a sermon in 1775 as "the fall of a towering structure which overwhelms numbers with its ruin".

No 36: The Panama Canal Scandal of 1892

The Panama Canal is a forty-eight mile man-made waterway which connects the Pacific and Atlantic oceans. When it opened in 1914, it substantially reduced journey times and avoided the necessity of sailing the treacherous seas around Cape Horn.

But its construction was far from plain sailing and was only completed when the Americans acquired the rights from the French.

The original French project was the brainchild of Ferdinand de Lesseps who, on the back of his success with the Suez Canal, was able to raise substantial amounts of money to fund the construction work, which began on 1st January 1881. Many of the investors were private individuals, some 800,000 in total of whom 15,000 were single women, and over the course of nine stock issues, a total of 1.8 billion gold francs was raised.

But the project was bedevilled by poor planning and the hostile terrain.

The jungle, through which the canal was to be cut, was rife with venomous snakes and mosquitos that welcomed the irresistible temptation of fresh blood. Yellow fever, malaria and other tropical diseases quickly made inroads into the workforce.

By 1884, the death rate was over 200 a month. Not surprisingly, the high death-toll put a bit of a dampener on the company's ability to recruit and retain experienced engineers. Much of the machinery, state-of-the-art steel shovels and diggers, rusted quickly, due to the damp, humid climate.

De Lesseps kept raising money through share issues, but the project was eating through cash and not making the progress that was anticipated. There was only one possible outcome.

On 4th February 1889, the Tribunal Civil de la Seine ordered the winding up of the Canal Company, which had spent an enormous $287m on the project, at the cost of some 22,000 lives. But the French government were reluctant to liquidate the company for fear of the impact on the investors and tried desperately to interest American companies in taking over the operation.

The extent of the scandal became apparent in 1892, when French nationalists accused a large number of ministers of accepting bribes from de Lesseps four years earlier to permit the last stock issue, even though it was obvious to those in the know that the company's finances were perilous.

Some 510 members of parliament were accused of receiving bribes from the Company to conceal its financial position from the public. De Lesseps, his son, Charles, the chief engineer Gustave Eiffel – heard of him? – and other members of the management were tried and sentenced to five-year imprisonment, although these sentences were later annulled.

One of the ministers, Bethaut, was sentenced to five years, of which he served three, and the main agent for the bribes, Baron Reinach, committed suicide. Some fled to England, while de Lesseps died in 1894.

The cross-channel ferry must have made a fortune from fraudsters, who were fleeing justice.

All of this was of little consolation to the 800,000 investors, who had lost their chemise as a result of the over-optimistic promises of a speculator and the avarice of their legislators.

The consequences were that there was a period of political instability and public trust in politicians was severely dented. Some commentators suggest that as two of the prominent characters in the scandal, Baron Reinach and Cornelius Herz, were Jewish, it helped stoke up the nascent French antisemitism movement.

In 1894, a new French company was set up to continue the work on a smaller scale and eventually in November 1903, under the Hay-Bunau-Vanilla Treaty, the United States took over its lease, shares and assets.

No 37: The Salad Oil Crisis Of 1963

This cautionary tale involves a notorious conman, Anthony De Angelis, American Express and Warren Buffett, amongst others.

Tino, as he was known to his friends, had already cut his teeth as a fraudster, taking advantage of the National School Lunch Act, by supplying two million pounds of uninspected meat to the Federal Government, overcharging them along the way. When the con was discovered, De Angelis went bankrupt, but he brushed himself down, picked himself up and started all over again.

Taking advantage of the Government's Food for Peace programme, designed to supply surplus goods to a Europe recovering from the ravages of the Second World War, he traded in vegetable oil products, cotton and soybeans from 1955. Seven years later, Tino was sufficiently established that he felt that he could corner the soybean market, by buying soybean oil on the futures market.

His plan was to drive up the price of vegetable oil, increasing the value of his contracts and enhancing the profits available to him from the futures market. Of course, Tino didn't have the financial resources to support his ambitious plans, so he used his large inventories of commodities to collateralise loans from banks and finance companies.

American Express had just opened up a new division, providing warehouses and, eager for stuff to store in them, wrote receipts for millions of pounds of vegetable oil, which de Angelis took to a broker, who promptly lent cash on the back of them; an easy way to get a pile of cash.

Naturally, American Express would want to satisfy itself that De Angelis actually had the vegetable oil that was collateralising the loans but the resourceful conman had thought of that.

Many of the tanks sitting in the Amex warehouse were full of water with only the minimum of oil floating at the top to satisfy auditors, who were carrying out spot samples; an old trick that I as a greenhorn auditor, with a fresh set of coloured pencils, was warned about in the late 1970s.

The other stunt Tino pulled was to connect each of the tanks with pipes so that, as the auditors made their way along the line, the oil was pumped from one tank to the other. By the time the con unravelled, De Angelis had loans from some fifty-one companies.

And unravel it did.

At its heyday de Angelis was claiming to have more vegetable oil than the Federal Government reported for America as a whole. Instead of inventories of $150 million, his company, Allied Crude Vegetable Oil Refining Co, had just $6m. The dozy auditors were tipped off and found that most of the tanks contained just water.

In November 1963, the bottom fell out of the futures market; the price of soybean oil falling from $9.875 to $7.75 in two days of trading, wiping out the value of de Angelis' loans. Instead of selling out at the top of the market and making good the deficiency in cash, Allied Crude had no alternative but to file for bankruptcy.

The market turmoil coincided with the assassination of JFK and the market went into freefall. One of the brokerages de Angelis used, Ira Haupt & Co, was left holding $450 million in securities and debts of $37m it couldn't pay and, as a consequence, it folded. Another, Williston & Beane, was bailed out by the New York Stock Exchange. De Angelis was declared bankrupt again and ended up in prison.

And where did the Sage of Omaha come in?

He bought a 5% stake in Amex at the bottom of the market, for $20 million, one of the first investments that made his fame and fortune.

One man's ill luck is another's good fortune, I guess.

PONZI SCHEMES
AND PYRAMIDS

FOR THOSE OF us who are lucky enough to have
some money to invest, we are always on the look-out
for schemes which offer a greater investment return than
is the going rate.

Before the days of financial regulation and, regrettably,
even after what was called enhanced investor protection was
introduced, this understandable desire to beat the market
provided a fertile ground for the scammer to operate in.

In this section, we will be looking at five examples of
what are known as Ponzi and pyramid schemes.

Before we start, it is worth pausing a minute to
understand the inherent features and flaws of these two
forms of investment vehicle. A Ponzi scheme takes its name
from Charles Ponzi (1882 – 1949), whose get-rich-quick

scheme collapsed in 1920 and, with it, went around $20m of his investors' hard-earned cash. The principal feature of a Ponzi scheme is that it pays an investor interest taken from the capital that they have invested or from the capital that others have paid in.

As a scheme, it has some longevity but will collapse, if a significant number of investors want to withdraw their cash at the same time. This usually happens when market conditions do not allow the managers of the scheme to pay the promised high levels of interest.

A pyramid investment scheme, on the other hand, is where new investors transfer their funds to the founders, or earlier members, and can only get a return by recruiting new members in turn. A pyramid scheme is entirely predicated on exponential growth and because of this inherent design flaw, can only result in the later subscribers, who are unable to recruit new members, losing their shirt.

No 38: William F Miller

The man widely credited with giving Ponzi his inspiration was Mr 520 per cent, William F Miller, who launched the Franklin Syndicate onto the unsuspecting world in 1899.

On 16th March, Miller, by then president of the Brooklyn church's Christian Endeavour Society, persuaded Oscar Bergstrom to hand over $10 to him to invest in the stock market, claiming he had access to inside information. In return for his money, Bergstrom received a signed receipt, which stated "the principal guarantied against loss. Dividends weekly from $1 upwards till principal is withdrawn."

You can't say fairer than that.

The way the scheme worked was fairly simple, establishing the classic modus operandi of a Ponzi scheme. The investor was promised a return of 10% per week on their investment, which was paid from the original deposit. They then had a choice of withdrawing the interest or reinvesting, but because the supposed returns were so eye-wateringly attractive, they would have been foolish to withdraw their principal. The scheme would only hit the buffers if the investors demanded all of their money back.

And success breeds success.

So delighted were some of the earlier investors that they persuaded their friends and colleagues to join; Miller's offer of 5% of the deposit of someone recommended to the scheme as commission no doubt helped. He advertised in 800 newspapers, spending some $32,000 of his investors' money.

And it worked.

By the end of the summer of 1899, Miller had twenty-two employees and the office in Brooklyn was stuffed with cash. Long lines of people waited patiently outside the offices, either to deposit or to receive their interest. At the scheme's height, there were some 12,000 subscribers and Miller was taking between $20,000 and $63,000 a day.

But there were a number of problems, aside from the inherent design fault, that would eventually spell disaster.

Firstly, Miller introduced a partner, Edward Schlessinger,

to the scheme. He was smarter than Miller and soon demanded his cut from the scheme. The gullible Miller obliged and Schlessinger squirreled his share away for the inevitable rainy day.

Then there was the problem of the receipts.

A third partner, Colonel Robert Ammon, a lawyer, was brought into the syndicate in October 1899 and his brain wave was to incorporate the scheme, offering a share for every $1 invested, provided the guarantee was surrendered. Miller could not help gilding the lily, because as well as promising a phenomenal 10% per week interest, he claimed that the value of the shares would quickly multiply.

The newspapers, whilst happy to accept Miller's adverts, wrote scathing articles about the shady, too good to be true scheme and the police were on the look-out for disgruntled investors. But none were to be found.

Inevitably, though, the brave public front could not be sustained and on November 24th, 1899, the three partners met at Ammon's offices to plot their escape. Schlessinger stuffed his share of the loot into a satchel, supposedly around $145,000 and fled, never to be seen again.

Bizarrely, Ammon persuaded Miller to put his share into Ammon's own bank account. By now a warrant was out for Miller's arrest and he fled to Montreal. Soon captured, he was brought back to the States to face justice and in 1900 was sentenced to ten years in prison.

Ammon put pressure on Miller to keep quiet about his involvement, paying his family a pension of $5 a week. Eventually Miller, by now ill with consumption (TB), gave evidence against the grasping attorney. In 1903, Ammon got his partial just desserts and was sentenced to four years imprisonment for stealing $30,500.

What eventually happened to Miller is uncertain. Some say that on his release, he ran a grocery store, whilst others say the consumption got him.

No 39: James Paul Lewis Junior

One of the remarkable features of Lewis' Ponzi scheme was that it defied gravity for so long. It is estimated that it lasted for around twenty years, during which time Lewis had collected around $800 million from his investors, Lewis being one of them himself.

His company was called Financial Advisory Consultants and was based in Lake Forest in Orange County, California. Many of his 5,200 clients were recruited by word of mouth, many through fellow churchgoers and church-based organisations. Initially, the minimum investment was $25,000 but as the fund began to start creaking, this was raised to $100,000.

Lewis span a good story, claiming that one of his funds delivered annual returns of 40%, while the other generated a more modest 20%. He was able to sustain such high levels of return, he claimed, by leasing medical equipment, financing purchases of medical insurance, making commercial loans and buying and selling distressed businesses.

To add a bit of glitz to the scam, Lewis claimed that his clients included a number of professional athletes and at least one movie star.

In reality, however, Lewis was paying the high levels of dividends from the investments of the newer recruits, as well as using some of the funds to finance a lavish lifestyle. Rather like George Best, he spent a lot of money on booze, birds and fast cars. The rest he just squandered. But the money kept coming in, many of his investors putting their life savings into a fund that promised returns that seemed too good to be true.

Of course, they were.

The writing was on the wall in 2003 when Lewis was unable to meet dividend payments. Investors became suspicious, but he placated them and bought some time by claiming that the Department of Homeland Security had frozen the funds. This, naturally, was bunkum and, when there was still no sign of the promised dividends, the FBI were invited to investigate.

Lewis did then what any self-respecting fraudster does when the net tightens around him – he fled.

An arrest warrant was issued on January 14th, 2004 and, after a narrow escape in Tallahassee, Lewis was arrested in Houston. The investigations showed the extent of Lewis' scam. Instead of the $814 million in clients' assets he was supposed to have had, his company's bank accounts held just $2.3m.

Even at the time that his funds were allegedly frozen, Lewis helped himself to $3 million and, amongst the assets the FBI seized, were five cars including two Mercedes and a BMW. A letter, dated sometime in 2001, showed that Lewis had speculated on high-risk currency trading; naturally, Lewis lost $6.5 million on that occasion.

On trial in 2006, Lewis received thirty years and was ordered to repay $156 million, Judge Carney calling the scheme a "crime against humanity" because many of its victims were elderly and had lost their life savings.

Only $11 million was ever recovered.

No 40: Charles De Ville Wells

Charles De Ville Wells (1841 – 1922) may be a relatively obscure figure these days but he has two major claims to fame: he was the man who broke the bank in Monte Carlo and perpetrated a massive fraud in France, which had all the hallmarks of a Ponzi scheme a decade before Charles Ponzi was in action.

An engineer by trade, Wells had an inventive mind – he designed a device to moderate the speed of a propeller, selling the patent for $5,000. But he soon turned his grey cells to more lucrative endeavours.

Around 1879, he turned up in France and launched a scheme, fraudulent of course, to raise money to build a railway at Berck–sur–Mer. He attracted a good number of investors, who never saw a return on their money. When the scheme unravelled, Wells fled with the money and he was convicted in absentia.

He next turned up in England where, from around 1885, he launched a scheme to fund some of his inventions, promising eye-watering returns. Monies were raised and, of course, no dividends were ever paid. One investor lost the modern–day equivalent of £1.9m.

Whilst in Monte Carlo in late 1891, he visited the

famous casino on a number of occasions. Each table had a cash reserve of 100,000 francs (the bank), and if a gambler won more than was available – a feat known as breaking the bank – play was suspended and extra cash was taken from the vaults in an elaborate ceremony. With a stake of around £4,000, Wells won £60,000, breaking the bank on a number of occasions.

Wells claimed he had devised an infallible system, although he was never able to repeat his success; others thought he had just had a phenomenal run of good luck but some, looking at his track record, have speculated that there may have been something underhand.

With some of his loot he bought a yacht and this proved his undoing. When moored in Le Havre, the yacht was raided, and Wells was arrested and extradited to England to stand trial for the fraud he committed in the patents scheme. He served eight years and then was imprisoned twice more, once in England and once in France, as the long arm of the law sought its revenge.

After his enforced rest, Wells popped up again, in 1910, under the alias of Lucien Rivier. He established a private bank in Paris on the Avenue de l'Opera, opening for business with the astonishing promise of offering a guaranteed 365% interest per annum. There was a ready audience for such enticing rates and investors scrambled to get a piece of the action. Wells was able to meet the interest payments of the early investors from the deposits paid in, the classic design feature of a Ponzi scheme.

The French authorities were suspicious of the bank's incredible claims and promises and began to make their enquiries. This caused panic amongst the investors. Inevitably, there were soon insufficient funds to meet the bank's obligations. Wells fled back to England with some of the money but, in 1912, he was arrested, brought back to France and imprisoned for five years.

Over 6,000 investors, depositing some two million francs, were stung in Wells' last scheme. So serious were the repercussions in the French banking industry that the authorities imposed stricter controls on private banks and subjected owners to more stringent vetting procedures.

Probably no bad thing but Wells had the distinction of breaking two different types of bank!

No 41: Sarah Howe

It would be wrong to give the impression that financial scamming is an exclusively male preserve.

Our next fraudster was a female and perpetrated her scam exclusively on the female sex. She operated in the 19th century and her get-rich-quick scheme had all the hallmarks of a Ponzi scheme.

Step forward, Sarah Howe.

Born in New England around 1826, Sarah moved to Nashville, where she married. The marriage did not last long, and she found herself a widow at the tender age of 24. Moving back to the Boston area, she held a number of jobs, none of which she was ostensibly qualified for, including working as a clairvoyant, a skill, which if she possessed it, would have been enormously helpful for managing someone's financial affairs.

Her light bulb moment came in April 1879, when she devised the Ladies' Deposit, a bank deposit masquerading as a charitable organisation, offering a safe home for funds belonging to women and which was to be exclusive to the female sex.

Investors were promised the astonishing return of 8% interest a month, allowing an investor to double their money in just nine months. Not unsurprisingly, she was inundated by deposits from single and wealthy females. At its height, the Deposit held funds of over half a million dollars, deposited by around 1,200 Bostonian women. Members had to be referred to the scheme by other members, a case of the sisterhood standing together, their initial deposit was a small one and under the rules of the scheme, they were only able to withdraw their interest earnings.

What this meant was that Howe was able to use the principal deposited to fund the monthly interest payments, ensuring that she was protected from the risk of a run of large capital withdrawals, although, according to her, the reason was to prevent them wasting their money on fripperies.

Perhaps a telling insight into her attitude to her investors.

This Ponzi scheme before Ponzi soon attracted the attention of the press. After all, it wasn't done for women folk to have access to a money-making scheme, which sensible chaps were precluded from. Sarah did nothing to hide her new found wealth and she bought a $50,000 mansion at no 2 East Brookline Street with a $20,000 down payment in cash. Miss Old Eight Percent, as she was known, was investigated by the *Boston Daily Advertiser* in September 1880. The paper claimed that Howe was unable to pay the returns advertised, in effect, declaring the scheme a scam, which prompted a demand from investors for their money back.

Howe decided to meet all demands, paying out $150,000 in interest and $90,000 in principal. But, inevitably, she could not hold the scheme together and when the monthly interest payments could not be made, the Ladies' Deposit was declared insolvent with some 800 investors losing upwards of $300,000.

The Boston authorities arrested Howe and so depleted were her finances that she couldn't raise the $500 bail. Charged with four counts of fraud, she spent three years in jail. But the enterprising Howe wasn't done yet.

On her release she set up an identical scheme, although this one offered a more modest 7% per month interest payment. Surprisingly, she raised $50,000 from the gullible, before disappearing once more, never to be heard of again.

No 42: The Albanian Pyramid Schemes

The transition from a state-run to a free economy can be a brutal affair, as events in Albania in the 1990s amply demonstrated.

In 1992, the Democratic Party of Albania, led by Sali Berisha, won the first democratic elections following the fall of the Communist regime. As a more free-market based Albanian economy began to develop, a number of superficially attractive fund companies began to spring up, offering members of the public significant returns.

Taking advantage of the newly won democratic freedoms, a relatively financially illiterate populace, and minimal regulatory supervision, these fund companies offered mouth-watering returns which seemed (and were) too good to be true in a country, where alternative forms of investment opportunities were limited.

The first scheme was that of Hajdin Sedjise, who fled to Switzerland later with several millions of dollars. This was then followed by the Sudja, run by a former shoe factory worker, Maksude Kadena, which offered interest returns of 100%. In all there were some twenty-three funds trading at the height of the boom.

So phenomenal was the success of the funds in attracting investors that many Albanians sold their houses, personal possessions, livestock and other assets to get a piece of the action. At their height, the Albanian pyramid schemes had two million of an overall population of 3.5 million investing in them.

The sheer size of the schemes and the ready availability of new investors masked the fundamental design flaw of a pyramid scheme for longer than might otherwise have been the case. As long as there were still people ready to join the bottom of the pyramid, the economic model would continue to provide returns to those higher up the pyramid. Of course, those at the very top of the chain would do very nicely, thank you. Despite external criticisms of what was going on, the Albanian government refused to condemn the schemes until it was too late.

Between 8th and 17th January 1997, the inevitable happened.

The schemes collapsed with debts of around $1.5 billion at a time when the average monthly income was $80. Naturally, there were lots of extremely peeved Albanians who had lost everything.

What happened next was extraordinary.

The population demanded that the government compensate them, and the country descended into chaos and anarchy. The government lost control of the south of the country and order was only restored in April 1997 thanks to the efforts of 7,000 troops supplied by the United Nations. By then, 2,000 citizens had lost their lives and Berisha his job. Lawsuits were filed against some of the fraudsters, many of whom had fled the country and were sentenced in absentia.

In terms of numbers of people involved, this was the world's biggest financial scandal.

Part Three

Hoaxes

CAUSING A STIR

SOME EXPLOIT THE credulity and gullibility of others in order to have a bit of a laugh at their expense, rather than to fleece them of their hard-earned savings.

To my mind, there is something appealing about an elaborately constructed hoax. I am full of admiration of those who have the cojones to pull off a massive stunt.

The four tales that follow are among my personal favourites.

No 43: The Berners Street Hoax Of 1810

Chaos descended upon Berners Street in London's Fitzrovia on 26th November 1810.

The road was crowded with merchants, who descended upon No 54, the home of a wealthy woman, Mrs Tottenham or, in some reports, Mrs Tottingham. *The London Annual Register* noted that what turned up included "Waggons laden with coals from the Paddington wharfs, upholsterers' goods in cart-loads, organs, pianofortes, linen, jewellery, and every other description of furniture." The poor lady of the house was at her wits' end.

During the course of the day, more and more tradesmen arrived, including an undertaker with a custom-made coffin. Around midday, the Lord Mayor of London arrived, brandishing a letter from Mrs Tottenham, asking him to favour her with a visit. He soon realised it was a fake and made a speedy exit, stage left.

The afternoon saw a steady flow of tradesmen and the street was in chaos with their carts. The scenes of confusion were made worse by a motley crew of onlookers, who had assembled to view the comings and goings. The police, in an attempt to restore order, blocked off both ends of the street, but it was not until it had grown dark that some sort of order was restored.

Each of the tradesmen had received a letter, purportedly from Mrs Tottenham, requesting them to attend her house with their wares at designated times during the day. As she was known to be a wealthy woman and of good standing, tradesmen jumped at the chance of doing some business with her.

Of course, it was all an elaborate hoax and the police were on the search for the perpetrator, offering a reward "for the apprehension of the criminal hoax."

The hoax generated considerable public interest and by the following year, references to it on the stage drew enthusiastic responses from the audience. The perpetrator, however, remained undetected.

By 1812, the finger of suspicion was pointed at a young writer of comic operas, one Theodore Hook, who was known as a playboy and practical joker. One of his favourite tricks, it seemed, was to knock on the front door of a perfect stranger and, using his charm and persuasiveness, secure himself an invite to dinner.

Hook made a confession of sorts in his semi-autobiographical *Gilbert Gurney*, published in 1835. In the book one character, Dray, remarks, "There's nothing like fun — what else made the effect in Berner's Street? I am the man — I did it."

Hook was never charged but further details of the possible motives for an elaborate hoax on a woman with whom he had no connection emerged in the early 1840s. It was said that, when he and a friend were walking down Berners Street, Hook pointed at random to Number 54 and said, "I'll lay you a guinea that in one week that nice modest dwelling shall be the most famous in all London."

It is even said that Hook and his accomplices, the sheer size of the hoax required that over a 1,000 letters be written and sent to tradesfolk, summoning them to Berners Street, rented a room across the way to better view the mayhem they had caused.

The hoax was not original. On 31st October 1809 a hoaxer had sent numerous tradesmen to the home of an apothecary in Bedford Street in Covent Garden as payback for some medicine "which did him no good" – but what marked it out was its sheer size and audacity or, as Grace and Philip Wharton put it in *The Wits and Beaux of Society* in 1861, "it was not the idea of the hoax — simple enough in itself — which was entitled to the admiration accorded to ingenuity, but its extent and success."

Quite.

No 44: The Great Bottle Hoax Of 1749

Human gullibility and credulity is a subject that has fascinated many for centuries.

A group of aristocrats, with nothing better to do than consider such points, met in 1749. The Duke of Portland opined that if the most impossible thing was advertised, "there would be fools enough in London to fill a play house and pay handsomely for the privilege of being there." The Earl of Chesterfield, after scratching his peruke for a while, thought that someone jumping out of a quart bottle would test the public's credulity.

And so the wager was struck.

An advert was placed in the London newspapers in the first week of January promising that, on 16th January at the New Theatre in Haymarket, there would be an exhibition by a performer who had already appeared before most of the crowned heads of Europe. The conjurer, as he was described, would take a walking cane from a member of the audience and play every instrument known to man upon it. Then he would take a common wine bottle which, after due examination by members of the audience, he would place on a table, jump into it and sing a selection of songs. Entry to this astonishing evening's entertainment would set you back five pounds.

London was agog and the forthcoming spectacle was the talk of the town.

All the tickets were snapped up. No one wanted to miss this extraordinary show. But when the audience had assembled, there was no sign of movement backstage. No entertainment had been provided to keep the punters amused before the show began and the audience became restless, starting to boo, stamping their feet and pounding their canes.

Eventually someone appeared on the stage and announced that, if the performance didn't start within the next quarter of an hour, the audience would get their money back.

Order of sorts was restored but as the quarter hour elapsed, there was still no sign that a performance was about to begin. Someone in one of the boxes grabbed a lighted candle and tossed it on to the stage.

This was the signal for a riot and soon seats were torn up and the frenzied audience proceeded to demolish everything within sight. The theatre was set alight and the more subdued members of the audience fought to make their exit stage left, leaving much of their portable apparel such as wigs, hats, and cloaks behind. A big bonfire was built outside the theatre and the stage curtains were made into an impromptu flag.

Even the cash receipts were taken.

The wags about town had a field day decrying the gullibility of the public. Some placed adverts, promoting feats even more ludicrous and impossible than the man in the bottle, some offering to rip out their own eyeballs or to jump down their own throats.

Another offered to shoot himself with two pistols, once through the abdomen and then through the brain. He promised that this tour de force would end "with staggering convulsions, grinning, etc., in a manner never before publicly attempted."

A story did the rounds that the conjurer had been prevailed upon by a certain gentleman to do a private performance. Once in the bottle, the gentleman put a cork into it and made off with him, hence his non-appearance.

The hoax, which sparked a riot, eventually ran out of steam, and the great British public diverted its attention to other affairs. It was some years before the perpetrators of the hoax were revealed.

No 45: John Howard And Mary Toft

We speak of people breeding like rabbits, but Godalming born Mary Toft (c1701 – 1763) took matters a whole lot further, she gave birth to rabbits, or at least so she claimed.

Despite having a miscarriage a month earlier, Toft still appeared pregnant and went into labour on 27th September

1726, giving birth to what seemed to resemble a liverless cat.

The Guildford based obstetrician, John Howard, was summoned and, upon his arrival, was presented with a number of animal parts, which Toft was said to have delivered during the night. The following day, Howard helped to deliver more animal parts and, over the course of a month or so, the astonishing Toft had produced from her womb the head of a rabbit, nine baby rabbits and the legs of a cat.

Realising that he had something on his hands that was too good not to exploit, Howard wrote to the great and the good, including leading surgeons and the King's secretary, informing them of the wondrous goings-on in Godalming. George I's interest was piqued, and the King sent his surgeon-anatomist, Nathaniel St Andre, and the Prince of Wales' secretary, Samuel Molyneux, to investigate.

By this time Toft's celebrity was such that Howard moved her into his own house. Astonishingly, Toft was still delivering body parts, in labour with her fifteenth rabbit by the time the King's men had arrived. Still their journey was not wasted as the indefatigable Toft gave birth to yet more rabbits, all dead of course.

St Andre examined some of the rabbits and, whilst it was unlikely that their internal organs could have developed inside Mary's uterus, he persuaded himself that he had witnessed some kind of miracle.

Others were not quite so gullible.

The German surgeon, Cyriacus Ahlers, was sent along by the King and witnessed several births. Examining one of the rabbits, Ahlers found that it had dung pellets containing bits of corn, hay and straw up its anus. He smelt a rat, or perhaps a rabbit, and reported back that it was a hoax, his suspicions further alerted by the fact that Mary adopted an odd posture, as if to stop something from dropping down from her midriff, and that Howard would not allow anyone to attend to her births other than himself.

On 29th November 1792, Mary, by now a national sensation, was brought to London. Large crowds would congregate around the house in which she was staying, effectively under lock and key. The mysterious births stopped and Mary's hoax started to unravel. Witnesses came forward claiming that they had procured rabbits on behalf of Toft. A porter was caught trying to sneak one into her room.

Threatened with a painful examination of her uterus by the eminent physician, Sir Richard Manningham, Toft confessed to the hoax. She had simply inserted the dead rabbits inside her womb when no one was looking and gave "birth" to order. Her motivation, it seems, was a desire for fame and, even, a pension from the King.

It is thought that when she miscarried in the August, she evacuated some placenta containing flesh or parts of the foetus. This gave her the idea to try and benefit from the personal tragedy.

For her sins, she spent a little time in prison for fraud but was released without trial. It is said that she gave birth to a normal child a year later, although you would have thought she would have had enough of matters obstetrical by then.

But for Messrs Howard and St Andre, the outcome was far worse – their medical careers were ruined. The satirists had a field day mocking their gullibility. William Hogarth's *Cunicularii* shows Toft in labour surrounded by the protagonists of the story.

No 46: H L Mencken And The Bathtub

Sometimes what is intended to be a bit of harmless fun gets out of hand and once the metaphorical cat is out of the bag, it is difficult to regain control.

A classic example of this is the curious case of the respected journalist and so-called sage of Baltimore, H L Mencken, and the history of the bathtub.

It was the dark days of December 1917. America had entered the First World War, something Mencken had opposed, and news from the front was dreadful. In order, as Mencken said later, "to have some harmless fun in war days", he wrote an article on the history of the bath tub, which was published in the *New York Evening Mail*.

In it, Mencken claimed that Adam Thompson had installed the first bath, made of mahogany and lined with sheet lead, in Cincinnati on 20th December 1843. This innovation in hygiene, according to Mencken, caused a storm, some attacking it as an example of epicurean luxury, whilst other medics claimed that bathing in this fashion was detrimental to one's health.

It was Millard Fillimore, claimed Mencken, who gave the bath a fillip. When Vice President, he visited Cincinnati, had a bath, felt no ill effects and quite enjoyed the experience. When he was elected President in 1850, Fillimore had one installed in the White House and the rest is history.

But of course, it wasn't; it was all bunkum and was a hoax designed to test the credulity of the general public and fellow journalists.

The fact that it was penned by Mencken, was well-written and seemed plausible, meant that the story had legs. To Mencken's surprise, his article appeared in a number of other journals and many papers printed abbreviated versions. It was then picked up by learned journals and histories of public hygiene and once it had taken root in the groves of academe, it was well-nigh impossible to shift.

Eight years later, Mencken decided to own up to his hoax, writing a front-page article for the *Chicago Tribune* on 23rd May 1926, entitled *Melancholy Reflections*.

In his apologia, he wrote, "This article… was a tissue of absurdities, all of them deliberate and most of them obvious..[it] was planned as a piece of spoofing to relieve the strain of war days and I confess that I regarded it, when it came out, with considerable satisfaction. It was reprinted by various great organs of the enlightenment, and after a while the usual letters began to reach me from readers. Then, suddenly, my satisfaction turned to consternation. For these readers, it appeared, all took my idle jocosities with complete seriousness. Some of them, of antiquarian tastes, asked for further light on this or that phase of the subject. Others actually offered me corroboration!"

He went on, "Pretty soon I began to encounter my preposterous "facts" in the writings of other men.. I began to find them in standard works of reference. Today, I believe, they are accepted as gospel everywhere on earth. To question them becomes as hazardous as to question the Norman invasion…"

In 1949, the exasperated journalist wrote, "Scarcely a month goes by that I do not find the substance of it reprinted, not as foolishness but as fact, and not only in newspapers but in official documents and other works of the highest pretensions."

The story wouldn't die.

Between his exposure of his own hoax and 1958, according to Curtis MacDougall, there had been thirty-eight instances of Mencken's story being presented to the general public as fact. It still persists. A Kia advert as recent as January 2008 for Soap on a Rope repeated the canard, without realising they had been had.

WHAT ON EARTH?

O UR APPETITE FOR novelty, the unusual, and the inexplicable knows no bounds.

These four hoaxes, all harmless fun, were designed to test the boundaries of human credulity.

No 47: Joseph Mulhattan

We live in an era of fake news, where it is hard to determine whether you are having your leg pulled or whether you are just being fed something to satisfy a prevailing political agenda. We have already seen that there is nothing new under the sun and this adage applies as much to fake news as to anything else.

The pre-eminent American hoaxer in the 1870s and 1880s was Joseph Mulhattan (c1853 – 1914); there are a number of variants of his surname, but this seems to be the most commonly accepted.

Mulhattan had no desire to profit from his pranks, just enjoying the thrill of the chase and seeing how long his hoax would run for and how many would fall for it. His Internet was the press. As the *Syracuse Sunday Herald* reported in December 1900, "He never made a cent by his lies and in ordinary business affairs he spoke the truth, but he had a mania for giving misinformation to the newspaper and indulged himself in the mania to the injury of his other business."

Joseph opened his hoaxing career by announcing to a startled world in 1877 that when George Washington's sarcophagus was opened up for repairs, the workers were greeted with the sight of a petrified President. "The features [were] perfectly natural ... the body is of a dark leathery colour, and may be said to be soft sandstone, which would likely break should an attempt be made to move it..."

Pure bunkum, of course.

Moving to Kentucky in the late 1870s, Mulhattan announced his arrival in the Bluegrass State by reporting the discovery of a giant cave near Glasgow Junction. It was at least twenty-three miles long, boasted three rivers, and mummified remains were found inside, he reported with his tongue firmly in his cheek. But the story took off. One local entrepreneur, J R Pucket, was so taken in by the hoax that he announced he was going to set up a steamboat service to take sightseers to view this marvel.

Joseph's flight of fancy, in 1880, concerned a young

girl, who was staying at the seaside and had been given a bunch of balloons. The wind got up and carried her off and, but for the presence of mind and steady aim of an old hunter, who shot the balloons one at a time and enabled her to return to terra firma unharmed, she would have been seen no more.

A charming but totally fallacious story!

In 1883, Joseph reported that a giant meteor had landed in Brown County in Texas, killing several cattle, destroying the home of herdsman, Martinez Garin, and imbedding itself 200 feet into the ground. So large was the meteor that it stuck out seventy feet into the air and resembled the Fort Worth court-house in design. The poor telegraphist at Brown County received hundreds of telegrams from reporters seeking more details.

In February 1887, Joseph reported to the *Kentucky Register* that a local farmer, one J N Parkes, had trained a troupe of monkeys to pick hemp. The story spread like wildfire and the *New York Times* printed an angry editorial denouncing the scab monkeys, noting that if the practice spread, honest labourers would be out of a job.

Poor Parkes, who neither had any monkeys nor grew hemp, started to receive hate mail and eventually persuaded the *Register* to print a retraction.

Mulhattan, despite being an ardent prohibitionist, was an alcoholic and his health declined, so much so that in 1901 it was feared he was on his last legs. *The Cambrian* printed an epitaph for him, ''Here lies what's left of liar Joe,/ A truly gifted liar,/ Who could outlie the liar below/ In realms of flame fire./ He lied in life, in death he lies,/

And if, his lies forgiven,/ He made a landing in the skies,/ He plays the lyre in heaven."

As ever with Joseph, not everything was as it seemed, and he hung on until 1914.

No 48: The Cardiff Giant Of 1869

On 16th October 1869, a group of workmen were digging a well behind a barn on the farm of one William C "Stub" Newell, when they made an astonishing discovery. They unearthed the petrified remains of a giant, ten-foot tall man.

News of the discovery spread like wildfire and crowds soon assembled, anxious to view the phenomenon. The enterprising Newell erected a tent over the site and charged a fee of twenty-five cents for a look. Two days later he upped it to fifty cents but even this did not deter the crowds.

The discovery was opportune as locally there had been an impassioned debate as to whether *the Bible* should be taken literally. One of the adherents of literalism had claimed that the passage in *Genesis 6:4* which states "There were giants in the earth in those days" was a historical fact.

The unearthing of the Cardiff Giant, as it was dubbed, seemed to have made his point. A group of businessmen clubbed together to raise $37,500 to buy the giant, so that it could be moved to Syracuse to be displayed more prominently.

Of course, the discovery was too good to be true because it was all an elaborate hoax, the brainchild of an atheist tobacconist from New York, George Hull – is there any other sort?

In light of the discussion on giants, he immediately "thought of making a statue, and passing it off as a petrified man." Not only would it give him the opportunity to pull the legs of the Bible bashers, it might even earn him some money.

The idea of an elaborate hoax was born.

Having secured a 3.2 metre tall block of gypsum, he had it carved by a German stonecutter, Edward Burghardt, based in Chicago. To give it the appearance of antiquity, the statue was treated with various stains and acids. It was then transported by rail to the farm owned by Newell, who happened to be Hull's cousin.

In all, Hull spent around $2,600 in setting up the hoax. The two workmen hired to dig the well, Gideon Emmens and Henry Nichols, were also probably in on the plot. One of the workers, on discovering the giant, remarked "I declare, some old Indian has been buried here!"

Despite the attempts to age the statue, they were extremely amateurish and didn't pass the scrutiny of experts. A palaeontologist from Yale University, Othniel C Marsh, declared it to be a fake. Chisel marks were plainly visible, which would have worn away had the statue been in the ground for any length of time.

Realising that he had had a good run for his money, Hull came clean and confessed that it had all been an elaborate hoax.

But the story of the Cardiff giant didn't finish there.

In a classic example of people believing what they want

to believe, the public didn't care that it was a hoax, they wanted to see it and kept coming in their droves. The giant was even given an affectionate nickname – Old Hoaxey.

Never one to miss out on a good thing, showman P T Barnum offered the owners of the giant $60,000 to lease it for three months. When they refused, he had his own replica made and displayed it in his museum in New York. The owners of the giant sued but the case was dropped when the judge wanted the genuineness of the original to be established.

The giant can still be seen to this day, housed in the Farmer's Museum in Coopertown.

No 49: The Great Chess Automaton Of 1769

If the doom-mongers are to be believed, the successful harnessing of artificial intelligence, never mind Mulhattan's trained apes, poses the biggest threat to employment prospects. Whether that will ever happen or whether some of the promised benefits of artificial intelligence will manifest themselves in my lifetime, only time will tell.

The game of chess has long been at the forefront of the battle for supremacy between man and machine, principally because its moves are regulated by a number of rules and it is a game of strategy and anticipation, testing the competitors' ability to think and plan.

World chess champion, Gary Kasparov, suffered a defeat in 1997 at the hands of an IBM computer called Deep Blue, although some doubts have been expressed as to whether conditions were fair for both contestants. These days, with increased computational power and more sophisticated programming, computers can regularly defeat even the strongest chess player.

The creation of machines to ape the behaviour of living creatures particularly fascinated the so-called Enlightenment thinkers of the 18th century and some astonishing examples have survived to this day.

But the machine which really swept Europe by storm was Baron Wolfgang von Kempelen's chess automaton, created in 1769. By all accounts it was a splendid affair, consisting of a large wooden box, stuffed full of wiring and gears, atop of which was a carved figure wearing, for exotic effect, Turkish clothing. When the mechanism was wound up, the Turk, as the figure was dubbed, would play chess against all comers.

It would move pieces by itself, develop strategy and reacted to the moves of its opponent, rather than just play in a predetermined way, irrespective of the circumstances. It was a remarkably successful player and regularly overcame opponents. Von Kempelen was moved to call it a thinking machine.

Von Kempelen took the automaton on tour around the courts and salons of Europe, challenging the great and good to pit their wits against the machine. The automaton rarely lost. One of its most famous scalps was that of Benjamin Franklin.

In 1790, thinking twenty years was a pretty good run, von Kempelen dismantled the machine. Following his death in 1805, his family sold it on to Johann Nepomuk

Maelzel who re-assembled it and took it out on the road. He even took it to America in 1826.

True to form, the automaton regularly won its matches.

There was intense speculation as to how the machine worked and secured its remarkable run of successes. To quell the obvious thought that there was someone in the box of tricks, von Kempelen would ostentatiously open up the box to reveal its innards before each show. The mystery piqued the interest of Edgar Allan Poe who, after witnessing a performance, wrote an article in which he claimed that there was someone in the figure of the Turk, rather than the box.

He was almost right.

The truth came out on 6th February 1837 in the *Philadelphia National Gazette Literary Register*. Von Kempelen and Maelzel had employed champion chess masters, who were secreted in the part of the box where the Turk came out. A series of sliding panels and a rolling chair hid them from view, whilst the innards of the box were being displayed, but once the box was shut, they moved back into the guts of the box. The chess masters could control the arms and hands of the automaton to ape their own hand movements and the use of magnetic chess pieces allowed them to see what was going on above their heads.

All in all, it was a rather clever hoax.

No 50: The Solar Armour Hoax Of 1874

One of the keys to military success is to ensure that your forces arrive at the field of battle in optimal condition.

When temperatures are at their height, it would be helpful if the soldiers had some apparel which cooled them down.

An article, published on 2nd July 1874 in Nevada's *Territorial Enterprise*, described the brainwave of a certain Jonathan Newhouse, who had invented solar armour. It seemed to offer a clever solution to the problem of perspiring soldiers.

The armour consisted of a long, closely-fitting jacket and a cap, both made of sponge, about an inch thick. A rubber sack was fitted below the right armpit, into which was poured cold water. There was a tube leading from the sack to the cap. Before setting out into the desert, the idea was that the soldier would saturate the sponge and then keep themselves moist by occasionally depressing the sack with their arm.

Having invented the armour, the intrepid Newhouse decided to put it through its paces, choosing the appropriately named Death Valley for the experiment.

Alas, for Newhouse, his invention worked too well.

A Native American tracker went to a nearby camp and indicated that the men there should follow him. About twenty miles from the camp, they saw Newhouse sitting against a rock in his armour, frozen and dead. His beard was covered in frost and an icicle, a foot long, hung from his nose. It seemed that he had been unable to remove the straps to the mechanism and after some time, his invention had killed him.

The story was soon picked up by newspapers in San Francisco and New York and even crossed the Atlantic, where the paper with the largest circulation in the world at the time, *The Daily Telegraph*, deigned to give it some column inches.

But something did not seem quite right about the extraordinary tale. Inventions were a bit Heath-Robinsonish at the time and it was true that a number of inventors had fallen off this mortal coil at the hands of their invention.

The Telegraph, in relating the tale, took a rather neutral stance regarding its veracity. Whilst acknowledging the fact that when you ice a bottle of wine by wrapping a cloth around it, the moisture caused by the evaporation is very cold, it would not go as far as accepting the circumstances of poor Newhouse's demise.

Perhaps, it was troubled by the twelve-inch icicle hanging from his nose.

Instead, rather like Herodotus, it was "not prepared to disbelieve it wholly nor to credit it without question."

Having got the story into so august an organ as *The Telegraph*, more details started to emerge of Newhouse's strange death. A further account of an inquest appeared in the August 30th edition of the *Territorial Enterprise*. There it was reported that strange chemicals in bottles were found in Newhouse's backpack. The court passed the verdict that "he fell victim to a rash experiment with chemicals with the nature of which he was imperfectly acquainted."

Of course, it was all an elaborate hoax and the truth eventually came out.

On the staff of the *Territorial Enterprise* at the time were Mark Twain and William Wright. The Solar Armour story was the work of Wright, better known as Dan de Quille, who in the 1860s was tipped to achieve greater literary renown than his colleague. The Solar Armour story was the creation of his fevered imagination and an experiment in to how far a ludicrous story would run.

Quite some distance, it would appear.

CONCLUDING THOUGHTS

THE OBSERVANT READER will have noted that the majority, but by no means all, of the scams and hoaxes presented here predate the middle of the 20th century. That is not to say that the art of scamming has died out.

Far from it.

The last couple of decades or so have seen some of the most egregious forms of corporate financial skulduggery ever known. I have just chosen to give some earlier examples to show that there is a long and ignoble heritage that today's fraudsters are following.

Some will argue that increased financial regulatory oversight, enhanced pharmaceutical testing requirements and more robust advertising standards have made the modus operandi of many of the individuals I have put into the spotlight redundant.

Up to a point, Lord Copper.

Regulators can only ever play catch up, leaving ample opportunities for the clever or determined scammer to exploit. And regulation tends to be national, whilst the worldwide web provides the opportunity to operate on a global basis. This, in turn, requires supranational co-operation to curtail their activities, always tricky to achieve at the best of times. No longer are their scams and hoaxes proscribed by the circulation reach of the journals they choose to deploy.

And then there is human nature.

Although we have access to more information at the click of a mouse than we ever had in the history of mankind, our knowledge base is built on foundations of sand. We take too much at face value, rarely questioning the provenance of or the reliability of the so-called facts that are presented to us.

The prevalence of fake news suggests that we are no less credulous than our forefathers. And some might argue that the 2016 UK EU referendum and the US Presidential election results show that gullibility is alive and kicking.

We are all aspirational, after all, and whilst we continue to be so, there will always be people willing to prey on and exploit our hopes and fears.

As a collector of scams and hoaxes I don't think I will run out of new material any time soon.

More about the author

If you enjoyed this book, check out Martin Fone's other books:

Fifty Clever Bastards – a study of luck and success or a simply a feast of schadenfreude, featuring fifty inventors who came a cropper; either they were killed by their inventions or were ripped off or simply gave their inventions away for the good of mankind.

Fifty Curious Questions – an attempt to answer some of those irritating questions that life throws up along the way. The selection is idiosyncratic and is designed to show the lengths scientists have gone to and the quantum leaps in logic they have deployed to push out the frontiers of human knowledge. The book was a Category Finalist in the prestigious 2018 Eric Hoffer Book Award.